the SOUTH'S BEST BUTTS

PITMASTER SECRETS for SOUTHERN BARBECUE PERFECTION

MATT MOORE

AUTHOR of
A SOUTHERN GENTLEMAN'S KITCHEN

S

ACE!

donnas

&

Keys

!

gnolia, TX

it all!

NG BACK

GUMBO!

WOW

TOUFFEE

Sausage & beef
Sooo! good.
Love the Boudain
too!

Steve &
Dianne

Enjoyed visiting
with Mr. Wallace
Johnson

Texas

HOW FOOD
SHOULD BE!

PARRAIN SPECIAL
RULES!!

Ray from
Chicago

awe
some

!!!

Best
After

GREAT
PLACE!!

Always
Great

A & J

Awesome!
St. Cloud, MN

Dan
Anderson

Omg! So
Good

I love
You never
forget that!

♡ -Madi

FROM SPRING
TEXAS

The BATES
Family

3/11/14

It was
delicious!
Angie

Amazing!
everything

Good
me
of the
r!

awesome!

glorious
(Oregon)

baked
was
UGLY
ould!

come
back

Hello GQ

-Breanna
Thibodeaux

Jessie Comeaux
♥'s
Johnsons!!

1st TIME
Smells Like
it won't be
the LAst

Ditto!!

MMM MMM!

Awesome keep up
THE GOOD WORK
AND GREAT SMELL

Louisiana
Golf Association
visits Johnsons
Boucanière all
the time!
Thanks for
great food!

As a first-timer here
I walked in and got
hit with a bomb-ass
Smell! Looking forward
to eating it at home!

Dirty D and
the boys.

love the food
thanks for
supporting local
businesses!
(the feedmseed)

Mac &
Cheese
should be
a lunch
Staple!

Great Bread Pudd...

My
Belly
Bunns with
Satisfaction

Please bring
back your
red beans,
delish

WE ♥
Johnsons
Boucanière!

Published by Oxmoor House, an imprint of Time Inc. Books
225 Liberty Street, New York, NY 10281

Senior Editor: Katherine Cobbs
Project Editor: Lacie Pinyan
Senior Designer: Melissa Clark
Photo Editor: Paden Reich
Location Photographer: Andrea Behrends
Studio Photographers: Iain Bagwell, Caitlin Bensel, Jennifer Causey, Greg DuPree, Alison Miksch, Victor Protasio, Christopher Testani
Prop Stylists: Jessie Baude, Kay E. Clarke, Paige Hicks, Mindi Shapiro Levine, Lindsey Lower, Amy Stone
Food Stylists: Torie Cox, Margaret Monroe Dickey, Katelyn Hardwick, Morgan Locke, Catherine Crowell Steele, Matt Vohr
Prop Coordinator: Audrey Davis
Recipe Developers and Testers: Robin Bashinsky, Mark Driskill, Tamara Goldis, Paige Grandjean, Adam Hickman, Elizabeth Laseter, Robby Melvin, Karen Shroeder-Rankin
Assistant Production Director: Sue Chodakiewicz
Assistant Production Manager: Diane Rose Keener
Copy Editors: Donna Baldone, Ashley Strickland Freeman
Proofreader: Polly Linthicum
Indexer: Mary Ann Laurens
Fellows: Helena Joseph, Hailey Middlebrook, Kyle Grace Mills, Natalie Schumann

ISBN-13: 978-0-8487-5185-2

Library of Congress Control Number: 2016959488

First Edition 2017

Printed in the United States of America

10 9 8 7 6 5 4 3 2 1

We welcome your comments and suggestions about Time Inc. Books.
Please write to us at:
Time Inc. Books
Attention: Book Editors
P.O. Box 62310
Tampa, Florida 33662-2310

Time Inc. Books products may be purchased for business or promotional use. For information on bulk purchases, please contact Christi Crowley in the Special Sales Department at (845) 895-9858.

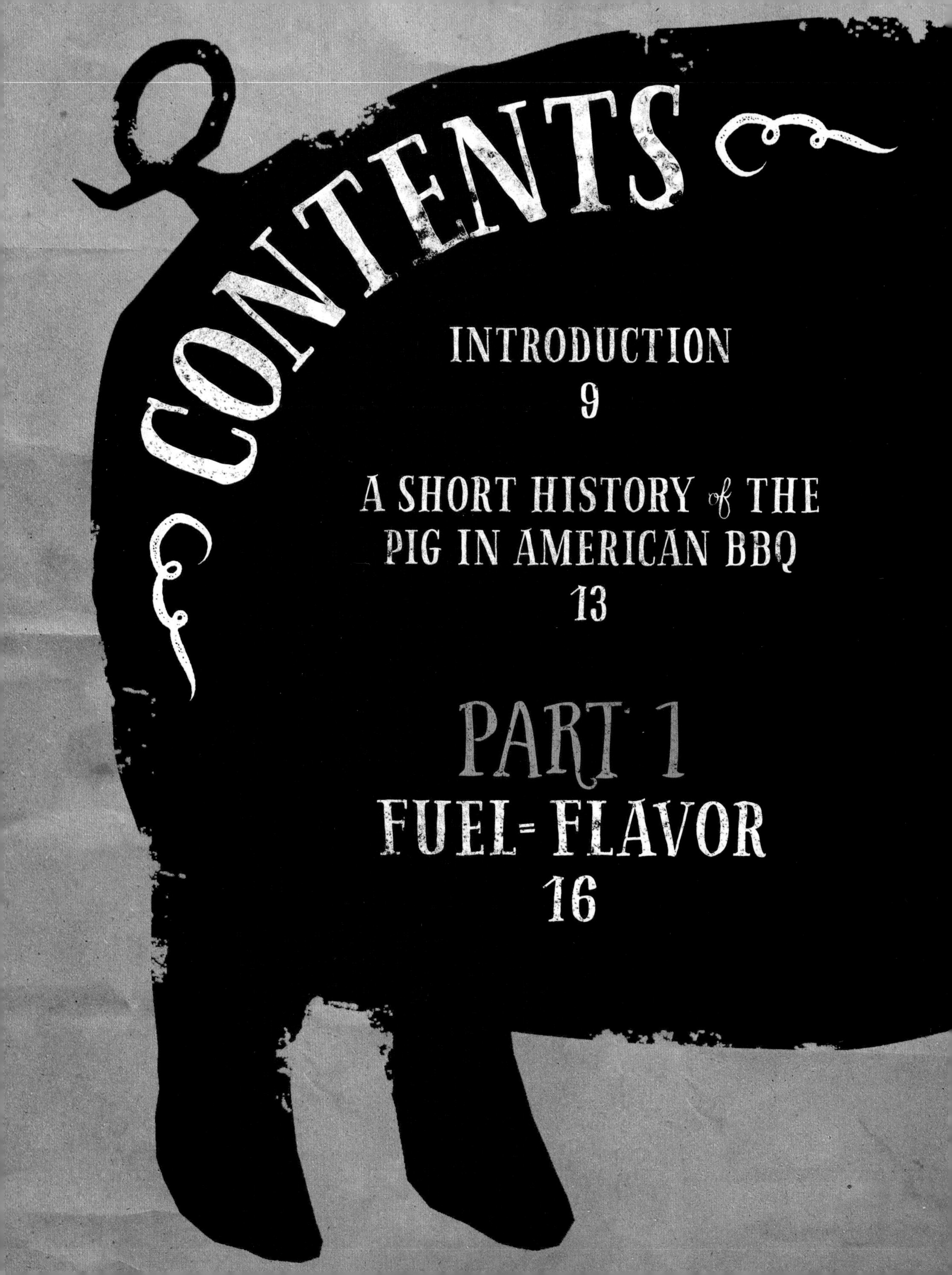

CONTENTS

INTRODUCTION
9

A SHORT HISTORY of THE PIG IN AMERICAN BBQ
13

PART 1
FUEL = FLAVOR
16

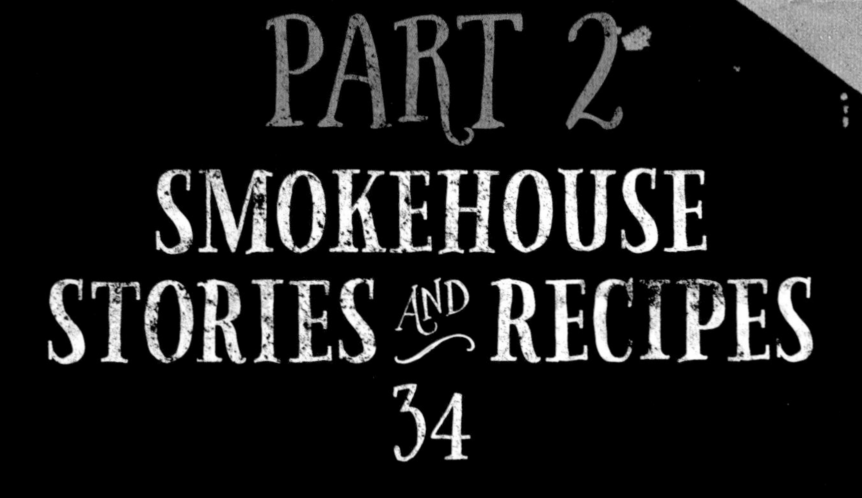

PART 2

SMOKEHOUSE STORIES AND RECIPES

34

PART 3

ALL the TRIMMINGS

170

ACKNOWLEDGMENTS 280

METRIC EQUIVALENTS 282

INDEXES 283

INTRODUCTION

OPINIONS ARE LIKE BUTTS—EVERYBODY HAS ONE. THE SAME COULD BE SAID ABOUT BBQ. AFTER ALL, THERE ARE AS MANY TYPES OF BBQ AS THERE ARE CHEFS. AND WHEN IT COMES TO GOOD 'CUE, EVERYBODY HAS AN OPINION. THROUGHOUT THE BBQ BELT, AND AMERICA FOR THAT MATTER, YOU WILL FIND COUNTLESS AND VARYING VIEWS, RECIPES, TECHNIQUES, AND TALL TALES THAT ALL PLAY THEIR PART IN THE RELIGION THAT IS BBQ.

Yes I said it, it's true. Southern BBQ is its own religion. And to experience it is akin to hearing the Gospel for the first time.

Smoke, perfumed with burning hardwoods, hisses and puffs out of open pits or smokers welded by hand. There's the faint sound of a sizzle, from time to time, as the slowly cooked meats gently self-baste, giving up their fatty goodness to flavor the fire. All the while, glowing embers snap and hum as they steadily smolder, releasing their hard-earned flavor that softly kisses the meat.

And then, of course, there are the pitmasters—men and women alike who serve as the grand conductors, or the preachers if you will, over the entire process. These folks hold as many secrets and hard-earned knowledge as they do good story and charm. At their basic level, pitmasters are perfectionists like no others—enduring years of trial and error to perfect their craft, often spending their entire existence smelling of smoke and meat while carefully drawing out the best of their 'cue during the hours when the rest of the world sleeps.

Creating BBQ is a humbling art—as it's not uncommon for nearly half a day's work to be devoured in minutes, and, of course, judged to the nth degree by said patron. That being said, no true pitmaster cooks seeking recognition from others. Instead, it is an inner desire, almost primal, if you will, to persistently stand among the smoke and the flames to bring out the most beautifully nuanced and delicious tastes beloved the world over. Like all things worthwhile in life, mastering the art of BBQ is, well . . . it ain't easy. One must constantly practice faith, persistence, and patience. But let me tell you, the rewards can be heavenly.

I've been eating BBQ my entire life. More specifically, I'll say that the consumption of slow-roasted pig in its various forms is my favorite form of gluttony. I say that not with a sense of pride, rather it's simply a way of life down here. If you cook BBQ, we will come, whether it's for a covered-dish supper, neighborhood gathering, tailgate party, political rally, or a wedding—yes, it's entirely appropriate to serve BBQ at a wedding.

FILSON
BOLOGNA

SIXPOINT
DALE'S
PALE ALE

Good 'cue never grows tiresome. In fact, I believe that some of my happiest moments in life could all trace back to a soundtrack of BBQ in the background—yes, even including my own wedding.

That said, I must offer up my first, of many, opinions. When it comes to BBQ, the pork butt reigns supreme in my book. Sure, I like a good side of ribs, pulled chicken, brisket, chipped mutton, sausage, and whatever other protein hits the smoke, but the pork butt is often my starting point for defining and enjoying good 'cue. It is humble, affordable, and forgiving. It can also stretch to feed a crowd. At the same time, the cut is extremely variable. After all, I've never come across a pork butt I didn't like, each one encompassing a different preparation, brine, rub, cooking technique, sauce, and method of service. The pork butt is ubiquitous, a veritable cornerstone of BBQ. As such, I felt compelled to travel throughout our fair South to visit and document the folks who pay homage to this cut—one state and one butt at a time.

So, I ask you to journey with me as we seek those men and women who keep the flames alive. Whether out on the open road or via the friendly skies in a '76 Piper Cherokee, I invite you to sit right seat as I provide a sneak peek into the kitchens, smokehouses, and personalities of the BBQ Belt's most enduring pitmasters—some known, and some you'll soon discover. We will explore the marriage of meat, preparation, method, and sauce from state-to-state-to-state. I will showcase the honest stories and delicious results that can result only from hours, days, and years spent coaxing meltingly tender perfection from the humble pig. Of course, your bellies will soon be grumbling, so I'll let you take the reins. I'll deliver the tried and true pork butt recipes I've managed to pry from these pitmasters, along with the trimmings, that will change the way you cook, smoke, grill, and eat.

Ready? Let's crack open a cold beer and get to work. I invite you to enjoy some of the South's best butts.

A SHORT HISTORY of THE PIG IN AMERICAN BBQ

THE STORY OF BBQ IN THE ANTEBELLUM SOUTH IS A BLEND OF HISTORY AND MYSTERY. THE TRUTH IS THAT A MYRIAD OF INFLUENCE, INGREDIENTS, CULTURE, AND YES, EVEN TECHNOLOGY ALL HELPED TO SPAWN AND SHAPE THE CRAFT.

For the Yankees, BBQ in the South is less verb and more noun. Barbecuing is not simply throwing meat on the grill and slathering it with sauce. As I, and others, will demonstrate in the pages that follow, barbecue takes more time, patience, and practice to perfect. So, be forewarned: if you invite me to a barbecue and you don't serve me slowly smoked pig (or other meats), I will refer to you properly and promptly as a Yankee. Whenever you grill your hamburgers, brats, pork chops, or steaks, do me a favor and invite me to a cookout or simply tell me you are grilling out . . . just don't call it barbecue, or barbecuing. Got it? Good.

And, now time for another opinion, which Texans (with their affinity for beef) and Kentuckians (with their love of neutrality and mutton) shall not take offense. True, Southern BBQ has one, and only one common denominator: pig. So let's dig in.

Generally speaking, historians and experts agree that domesticated pigs appeared in China around 5000 B.C. Thousands of years later, the Romans played their part by experimenting with pig breeding, resulting in the spread of pork production throughout the empire. While new breeds were brought to life, the pig also faced laws and bans by predominant religions throughout the world—many of which are still in place today.

It is written that Christopher Columbus, with encouragement from Queen Isabella, first brought pigs to Cuba in 1493. The resiliency and low maintenance of the animal, not to mention their potential as a food source, made them a natural fit for long journeys at sea. It was Hernando De Soto, however, who is most likely the man who deserves the most credit for bringing pigs to America when he arrived at Tampa Bay, Florida, in the mid-1500s.

So what's in a name? Here's where the history and mystery comes into play. Many historians, citing 15th century Spanish texts, trace naming rights to the term *barbacoa,* which loosely describes a method of using spits to roast meats over hot coals. Others give partial credit to the Haitians, citing the French phrase *barbe à queue,* another rough translation meaning head to tail (beard to tail for the Francophiles), describing the method of whole-animal cooking, especially practiced throughout the Carolinas. My unlikely favorite, as referenced by barbecue expert Daniel Vaughn, stems from modern

19th century advertisements, documented by *TarHeel Magazine* in 1982, using the moniker BAR-BEER-CUE-PIG. Using just a few words, the advertisement tells folks what awaits them inside—a miraculous combination of whiskey bar, beer parlor, pool hall—and hawker of slow-roasted pig. Paradise, if you ask me. In any event, I'm not a historian. All I know is that good BBQ is damn good delicious.

For centuries, the pig has remained a universal fixture of the Southern landscape and diet alike. Unlike raising domesticated cattle, hogs could be successfully raised at reduced costs, on less than desirable grounds, and with much less attention. The method of slow-cooking and indirect heat technique used to cook these animals allowed less desirable, and most notably, less expensive cuts to be transformed into a tender, delicious delicacy.

It's no surprise we Southerners have long been praised for being resourceful—not letting anything go to waste. Some folks, Yankees especially, say we'll eat almost anything, which is partially true. Pork has certainly helped play its role in keeping the South alive during times of need, including the Civil War, as preserved salted pork atop a hardtack biscuit was consumed for many-a cheap meal when times were tough.

In better times, the act of slaughtering a pig is a time of celebration, when entire families gather to do the work of butchering, cooking, and preserving every part of the animal. During the plantation era, the pig also broke the bounds of social hierarchy. In a rare act of humanity, plantation owners often threw feasts, known as pig pickin's, for slaves. Times, rightfully so, have changed. However, the pig's role in racial, social, and economic status should not be dismissed. The pig, and its consumption, is devoid of discrimination. On the whole, everybody is invited to celebrate in the feast. Ah, the power of the pig!

An unlikely player, the automobile, played a significant role in spreading and defining the 'cue establishments that we so knowingly love in modern times. Prior to such technology, most BBQ establishments were worked by farmers, as a weekend hobby or a means to supplement income. Cinder block shacks still adorn the Southern countryside—places where folks constantly tended the fire and prepared their repast. Since most pits were filled with smoke and soot, BBQ was often eaten as an on-the-go, cheap, and road-friendly meal. Going for a "Sunday drive" took on new appeal, as folks would travel to different pits along the road to taste and discover each pitmaster's distinctive creations, thus spawning the never ending argument as to whose 'cue reigned supreme.

Over time, the shacks evolved into actual eating places—encouraging folks to sit down and enjoy their food. This created a place where people of nearly every color and class could enjoy a meal, a welcomed reversal of the Jim Crow traditions at the time.

Let us not omit politics—something every Southerner knows to never discuss at the dinner table. Though barbecue has long served as a staple at covered-dish suppers and after-church picnics, it also widely appears at political rallies. I like to think that talk is cheap—and so are politicians—and, well, so is BBQ. To garner crowds, and potentially political favor, barbecue suppers are often thrown by politicians to help savor and spread their platforms.

There is no doubt that BBQ remains a relevant and preserved icon of Southern foodways and culture. Though establishments today might have become more fanciful, the hard-earned method, traditions, and techniques of the past still remain a relevant form of preparation and preservation for any notable establishment. Certainly, who makes the best BBQ is always worthy of a good debate. I can confidently say such debates and arguments will continue to dominate Southern conversations for the foreseeable future.

Rather than argue, I say we eat.

BOGART'S SMOKEHOUSE
ST. LOUIS, MISSOURI
PEAK BROTHERS BAR-B-QUE
WAVERLY, KENTUCKY
BURN CO. BARBECUE
TULSA, OKLAHOMA
BIG BUTTS BBQ
LEACHVILLE, ARKANSAS
HELEN'S BBQ
BROWNSVILLE, TENNESSEE
WILBER'S BARBECUE
GOLDSBORO, NORTH CAROLINA
SHULER'S BARBECUE
LATTA, SOUTH CAROLINA
SQUEALER'S
HICKORY SMOKED
BAR-B-QUE
MERIDIAN,
MISSISSIPPI
BUTTS TO GO
PELL CITY, ALABAMA
HEIRLOOM MARKET BBQ
ATLANTA, GEORGIA
JOHNSON'S
BOUCANIÈRE
LAFAYETTE,
LOUISIANA
B-DADDY'S BBQ
HELOTES, TEXAS

PART 1

FUEL = FLAVOR

FUEL=FLAVOR

I'VE ALREADY ESPOUSED MY OPINION ON BBQ VS GRILLED MEAT, BUT LET'S SPEND A BIT OF TIME LEARNING ABOUT THE DIFFERENCE AND SIMILARITY BETWEEN THE TWO. GRILLING IS LOOSELY DEFINED AS BROILING. SINCE MOST OF US ASSOCIATE BROILING WITH OUR OVENS, THINK OF IT IN THIS MANNER: GRILLING MEANS DIRECT HEAT FROM BELOW.

COOKING OVER COALS ON A GRILL

The direct heat method involves placing the food over the heat source. Consider the sizzle of steaks when placed directly over the coals or crisping up chicken wings until you get that crunchy skin, and, of course, getting a nice sear on that juicy hamburger. That, my friends, is direct heat grilling. For our purposes, let's make it easy on ourselves—direct, high heat will be referred to as grilling from henceforth.

COOKING BESIDE COALS ON A GRILL

To create delicious pork butts and other forms of BBQ, we utilize a different method of grilling by offsetting the food from the heat source, otherwise known as cooking by indirect heat. This can be accomplished in two ways—either vertically (placing the meat high above the heat source, often separated by a liquid or smoke layer) or horizontally (placing the meat offset from the heat, either away from the coals on a traditional grill or by utilizing a firebox or chamber setup on a smoker).

OPEN PIT

So, is it possible to craft on a grill using direct heat? Well, yes, but let me explain. Many folks in the Carolinas and western Tennessee still embrace an open pit technique. This originally started when folks would literally dig an open pit into the ground to roast a whole hog. Nowadays, in the restaurant environment, you will find open pits built with thick cinder block walls and iron bars or steel grating to hold the meat. The wood is burned down to coals in barrels typically away from the pit. The glowing coals are then shoveled into the pit and spread underneath the meat. The meat is sometimes covered by sheet metal to retain the heat, or the pit is otherwise left open, hence the name. The idea is that as the meat cooks, its juices slowly fall to the glowing embers underneath, which sizzle and pop, while also perfuming the meat with a whole new addition of smoke and flavor. Technically, this is direct heat—although most of these open pits typically place the meat with a good bit of vertical distance from the coals, which by definition, could also satisfy the indirect method. Now are you starting to understand why everyone has an opinion or two on good BBQ?

Opinions aside, let me tell you something: The day you decide to dig a pit in the yard, roast a pig through the night, and have friends over for a pig pickin'—that, my friends, is a day of celebration.

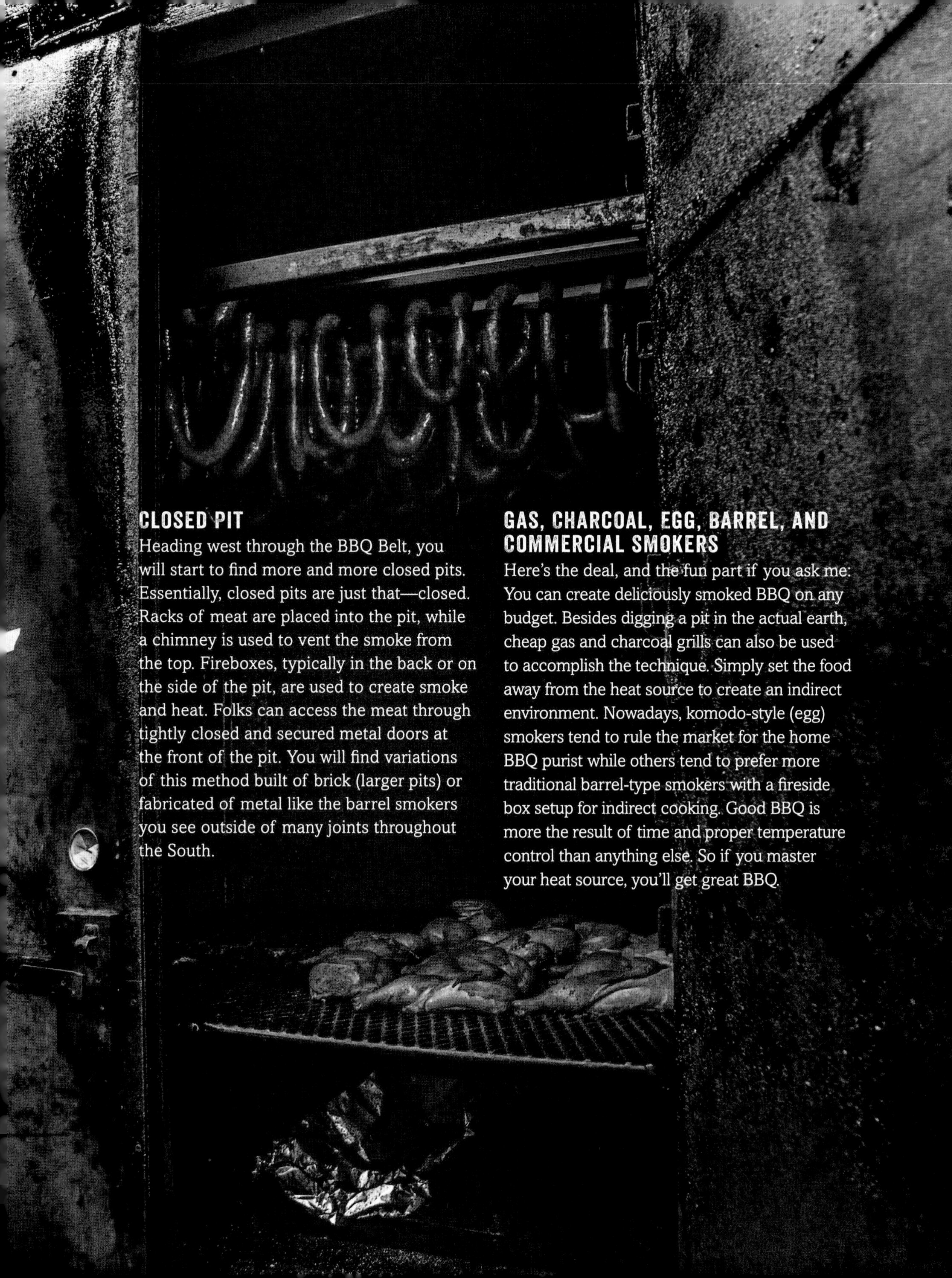

CLOSED PIT

Heading west through the BBQ Belt, you will start to find more and more closed pits. Essentially, closed pits are just that—closed. Racks of meat are placed into the pit, while a chimney is used to vent the smoke from the top. Fireboxes, typically in the back or on the side of the pit, are used to create smoke and heat. Folks can access the meat through tightly closed and secured metal doors at the front of the pit. You will find variations of this method built of brick (larger pits) or fabricated of metal like the barrel smokers you see outside of many joints throughout the South.

GAS, CHARCOAL, EGG, BARREL, AND COMMERCIAL SMOKERS

Here's the deal, and the fun part if you ask me: You can create deliciously smoked BBQ on any budget. Besides digging a pit in the actual earth, cheap gas and charcoal grills can also be used to accomplish the technique. Simply set the food away from the heat source to create an indirect environment. Nowadays, komodo-style (egg) smokers tend to rule the market for the home BBQ purist while others tend to prefer more traditional barrel-type smokers with a fireside box setup for indirect cooking. Good BBQ is more the result of time and proper temperature control than anything else. So if you master your heat source, you'll get great BBQ.

FUELING THE FIRE

Where there's fuel, there's fire—that's what we are looking for. When it comes to an actual heat source, you have endless options, with the oldest and most common being wood. That's right, that same wood you'll be using to provide smoke and flavor can also be used as your heat source. That's the way the cavemen did it—and so can you.

That said, you don't want to simply light dry wood and place food into the flames. You want the wood to burn down into coals—this is usually done away from the pit—and use the burned coals as your source of heat.

If you do not want to go through that much effort, charcoal serves as the most common fuel. I prefer lump, natural charcoal over briquettes. Honestly, don't use the briquettes unless you are absolutely out of other options. There's much debate over the chemicals used in briquettes and also their tendency to impart a metallic flavor. I skip the debate and use lump, natural charcoal instead. Instead of using lighter fluid, I prefer to light my lump charcoal using either a chimney or electric starter.

CLASSIC METHOD

Lighting all the charcoal at one time and adding it to the grill or smoker is known as the classic method. Essentially, you want to light enough charcoal as necessary to get up to and maintain proper temperature. Over time and for longer cooking periods, you will need to add more lit coals. The problem with this method is severalfold. Lighting all the coals at one time means that most likely the fire will be too hot. You will be closing off the air supply to prevent the fire from roaring out of control. Lighting all the coals also means that you will get less burn time, which means you will be continually opening and closing the grill (letting go of all that precious smoke, moisture, and flavor) to refuel the fire.

MINION METHOD

My preferred manner when utilizing charcoal is known as the Minion method. This method is most often utilized on kettle and komodo-style smokers. Instead of lighting all of the coals at one time, you light just enough of the coals and place them in contact with unlit coals. The idea, and with proper air flow, is that the lit coals will slowly burn and light the remaining coals in a steady, uniform pattern. I like to achieve this by creating a "reverse volcano" inside the bowl of my smoker. I stack fresh lump charcoal with the larger pieces towards the bottom around the perimeter of the bowl, leaving a hole in the bottom of the pile. Imagine placing a road cone inverted into the center of your smoker, filling the charcoal around it, and pulling it out. You get a reverse volcano! From there, I light just a few larger coals in the chimney starter and add them directly into the bottom area of the smoker. Using the vents on the smoker, I maintain just enough airflow for the coals to slowly burn outward, providing me with smoking times of nearly 15 to 20 hours, depending on the quality of the grill and charcoal.

THE HYBRID METHOD

That said, natural wood and charcoal are not your only two options. Most folks are accustomed to using grills that support either propane or natural gas. Guess what, that works too! Although, I will say, the purists believe it ain't BBQ unless it's cooked with wood and only wood. Nowadays, many pitmasters use large gas-assist cookers made by known manufacturers such as Southern Pride or Old Hickory. I say gas-assist as these pits typically control the heat in the pit using gas, while the smoke flavor comes from fireboxes that burn actual hardwood logs.

An advantage of using gas as a heat source is that you can maintain a steady, constant temperature without as many distractions. In this instance, and depending on your grill, you simply want to offset the food from the heat source. For those with standard backyard grills, use only one or two burners, and place the food on the unlit side, then cover the grill, and let the time tick on.

TAMING TEMPERATURE

So, now that we've got the pit chosen, along with a source of fuel, it's all about temperature. Learning how to steadily control temperature over time is what will allow you to become your own pitmaster, of sorts. We've already discussed several sources of fuel including wood, charcoal, and gas, but there's one more ingredient missing from the mix—oxygen.

Most grills and smokers provide you with two oxygen controls—typically an intake damper towards the heat source and an exhaust damper at or near the top. The intake (bottom) damper truly is the make or break control, allowing oxygen to either ignite the fire to its full potential or to extinguish the fire altogether by cutting off the supply. The exhaust (top) damper plays an equally important role by allowing gases, heat, and smoke to exit. If you've ever tried to fill up a lawnmower using one of those red gas tanks without opening the small vent opening, you'll notice the gas will pour, then suck, then pour. Opening that small vent will provide an even, steady stream. That's the same concept with the exhaust damper. Not only does it allow things to escape, but it also provides the draft, which pulls oxygen into and out of the smoker.

Obviously, the more oxygen you allow into the smoker, the more the fuel will combust, releasing more heat. Want to grill a steak? Open 'er up all the way. Want to smoke that brisket for 16 hours? Give 'er just enough oxygen flow to keep the fire alive at a steady 225°F.

So, what's the right temperature? That, my friends, is where I make my living. Remember what I said about opinions earlier? That's right—everybody has one. As you will soon discover in the profiles ahead, pitmasters have their own fiercely debated opinions on nearly every aspect of the BBQ process. Time and temperature are usually the most hotly (no pun intended) debated.

In general, and I can't believe I'm committing myself to this in writing, I see smoking temps vary from 200°-325°F for good 'cue. Obviously, the lower the temp, the longer the cooking time and vice versa. Some folks swear by super low temps over extremely long periods. I've seen (and eaten) ribs smoked low and slow for 6 hours at 200°F, and I've also had them grilled hot and fast over direct heat at 400°F. Both were delicious. Both were different. Agree to disagree if you have an opinion.

WHEN FUEL IS FLAVOR

Moving on to the smoking aspect. Where there is smoke, there is flavor.

An array of woods and techniques allow you to use smoke as the two-punch to add deliciously nuanced flavor to the meat. Finding the balance of not too much and not enough is something that takes time and practice, and also preference. Some folks tend to love the strong smoke flavor of hickory or mesquite while others opt for fruit and nut woods that provide a milder smoke flavor.

Meats absorb the most smoke flavor during the first hours of cooking. Most great pitmasters will control the smoke flow to impart its most impact during this time. Notice I said smoke flow. You never want the smoke to stagnate; instead, you want to open the vents or damper just enough to keep a steady flow of smoke passing through your cooking device during the smoking period. Think about your own experience eating great BBQ. Do you remember that pink ring just inside the charred outer crust of a slice of tender Texas brisket? If you do, then the pitmaster certainly did a job well done.

To get smoke, you need wood. A variety of fruit-, nut-, and hardwoods can be utilized to smoke foods, the most common being hickory, mesquite, alder, oak, pecan, walnut, maple, cherry, plum, apple, and peach. These woods can often be found in a variety of different textures, from dust to pellets to chips to chunks. A hard and fast rule is that certain woods produce more mild smoke flavors, while others are stronger.

MILD SMOKE: alder, maple, peach, plum, apple, cherry
STRONG SMOKE: mesquite, hickory, oak, pecan, walnut

Whatever you do, avoid any softwoods such as pine, spruce, or cedar. Keep in mind that natural, air-dried wood is preferred. Fresh-cut (green) wood is not ideal because the sap and moisture content can alter flavor and temperature. Avoid using any woods with mold or insect damage. And lastly, never use processed lumber, seriously. It's altered with chemical compounds that are not only dangerous to burn but also can affect your health.

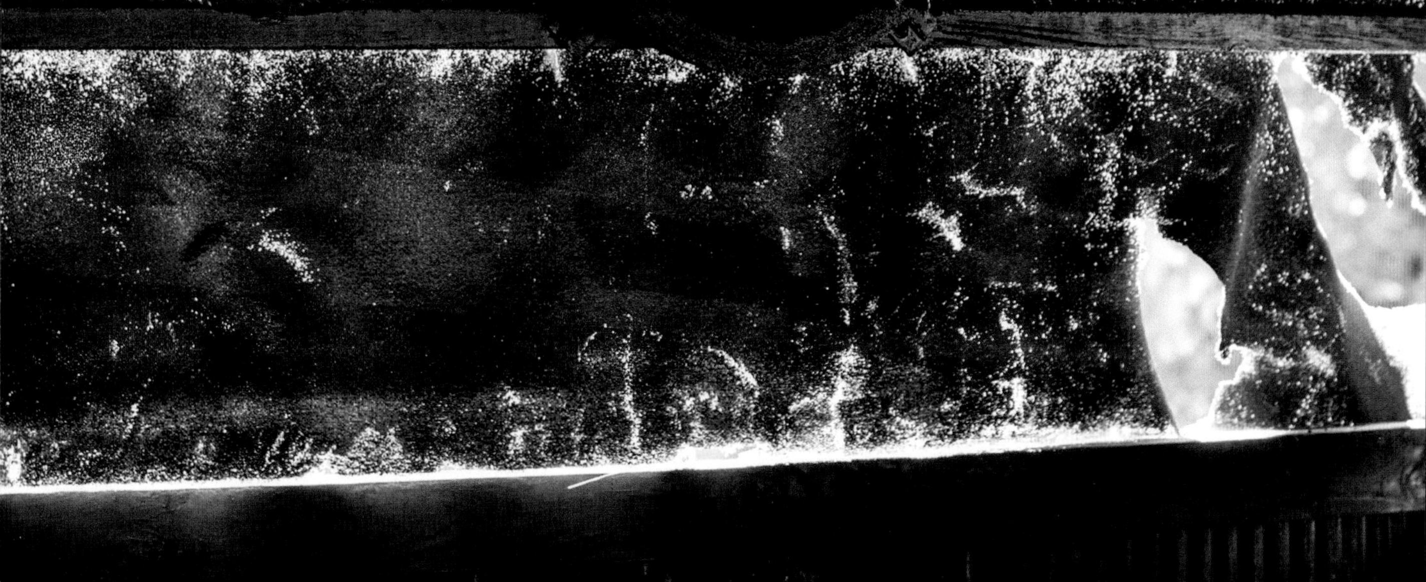

the FIVE MOTHER SAUCES

AS A KID, DADDY ALWAYS TOLD ME THAT LEARNING HOW TO BECOME GREAT AT SPORTS MEANT THAT I HAD TO FIRST MASTER—AND ALWAYS PRACTICE—THE FUNDAMENTALS. MUCH IS THE SAME WITH COOKING—AND WE OWE A LOT TO THE FRENCH IN TERMS OF FUNDAMENTALS—KNIFE SKILLS, BUTCHERING, BRAISING, BAKING, ROASTING. BUT THERE'S PROBABLY NO OTHER FUNDAMENTAL THAT EPITOMIZES FRENCH GASTRONOMY MORE THAN CRAFTING A SAUCE. HELL, THEY EVEN HAVE THEIR OWN NAME, "SAUCIER," FOR THE FOLKS WHO SPECIALIZE IN THEIR MAKING. AS SUCH, THE FRENCH DEFINED FIVE MOTHER SAUCES FOR GASTRONOMY: TOMATO, HOLLANDAISE, BÉCHAMEL, ESPAGNOLE, AND VELOUTÉ.

Though Southern BBQ has little to do with French gastronomy, it does share a commonality in terms of mother sauces, very loosely defined by five of its own: vinegar, sweet, mustard, white, and black. The sauces pair well with each region's distinctive dish—and there are as many variations on sauces as there are opinions.

I thought it prudent to garner some expertise from a longtime buddy and sauce expert Michael McCord. Michael and I have been friends for nearly two decades, first meeting when we were deciding upon our colleges of choice. Fortunately, for the both of us, we decided to part ways, me attending the University of Georgia, he choosing to cross state lines to go to Auburn University. Had we gone to the same school, neither of us would probably be alive today.

After school, Michael took his long-term love of BBQ and put it into business—founding Firebud Brands out of his home in Atlanta. His signature "Slap Sauce," a mustard-based concoction, soon caught on, along with his over-the-top, friendly personality. Today, Michael's sauces, rubs, and charcoals are distributed throughout the South—a true testament to entrepreneurship and creativity.

Walter Thompson

So, here are the do's and don'ts when it comes to sauce and BBQ, along with recipes for the five mother sauces.

It's important to note that BBQ sauce should not take away from the meat's leading role but should play supporting cast and give the main character more depth, more symmetry, or (gasp!) save that overcooked morsel that went unnoticed on the grill.

As Michael notes, there are three unwritten commandments of barbecue sauce. To break any of these cardinal rules would be akin to not holding the door open for the elderly, answering your phone in a crowded elevator, or wearing white after Labor Day.

1. NEVER under any circumstance use Liquid Smoke to add that char-smoke flavor. Any pitmaster worth his salt knows the true meaning of slow and low cooking, and this includes imparting the perfect amount of smoke into their meat. Whether it be hickory, mesquite, post oak, etc., let real wood take care of this aspect during the cooking process. This should go without saying, but you'd be surprised.

2. ALWAYS serve the sauce on the side. Let your guests determine how much (if any) sauce they wish to have drizzled over, slathered on, or dipped into their 'cue.

3. BALANCE your flavors within your BBQ sauce. Just like wine, there should be a yin to the yang. Making a sweet red sauce? Balance out the sweetness with a touch of vinegar. Experimenting with a true mustard sauce? Harmonize your taste buds with a dollop of tomato paste.

THE COUNTRY'S QUILT OF 'CUE

From the Lowcountry of the Atlantic to the Gulf of Mexico, and bordered by Texas and Missouri, the BBQ Belt encompasses the following states: North Carolina, South Carolina, Georgia, Tennessee, Alabama, Mississippi, Louisiana, Arkansas, Missouri, Texas, and Oklahoma. For the most part, pork rules in all of the preceding states, with the exception of Texas, where beef rules; Oklahoma, also a notable beef state; and Kentucky, known for its barbecued mutton.

Sauces also vary throughout the BBQ Belt. Sauces in the coastal areas bordering the Atlantic, most specifically North Carolina, are primarily vinegar-based. Working your way west, mustard sauces begin to appear, largely in part due to the French and German immigrants who first settled the area. Northeastern Kentucky produces a sauce that's dark, or black in hue, with the notable affinity for Worcestershire. North Alabama combines vinegar and mayo (along with a slew of variations) to produce a chalky white-style sauce. And finally, Tennessee and Kansas City BBQ are known for tomato-based sauces sweetened with molasses. In terms of the rest of the geography, you can basically count on a hodgepodge of variations from the core sauces, along with more spice, sweetness, more/less vinegar, so on and so forth. In some places, such as Memphis, it's dry rub. Sauce is mostly frowned upon.

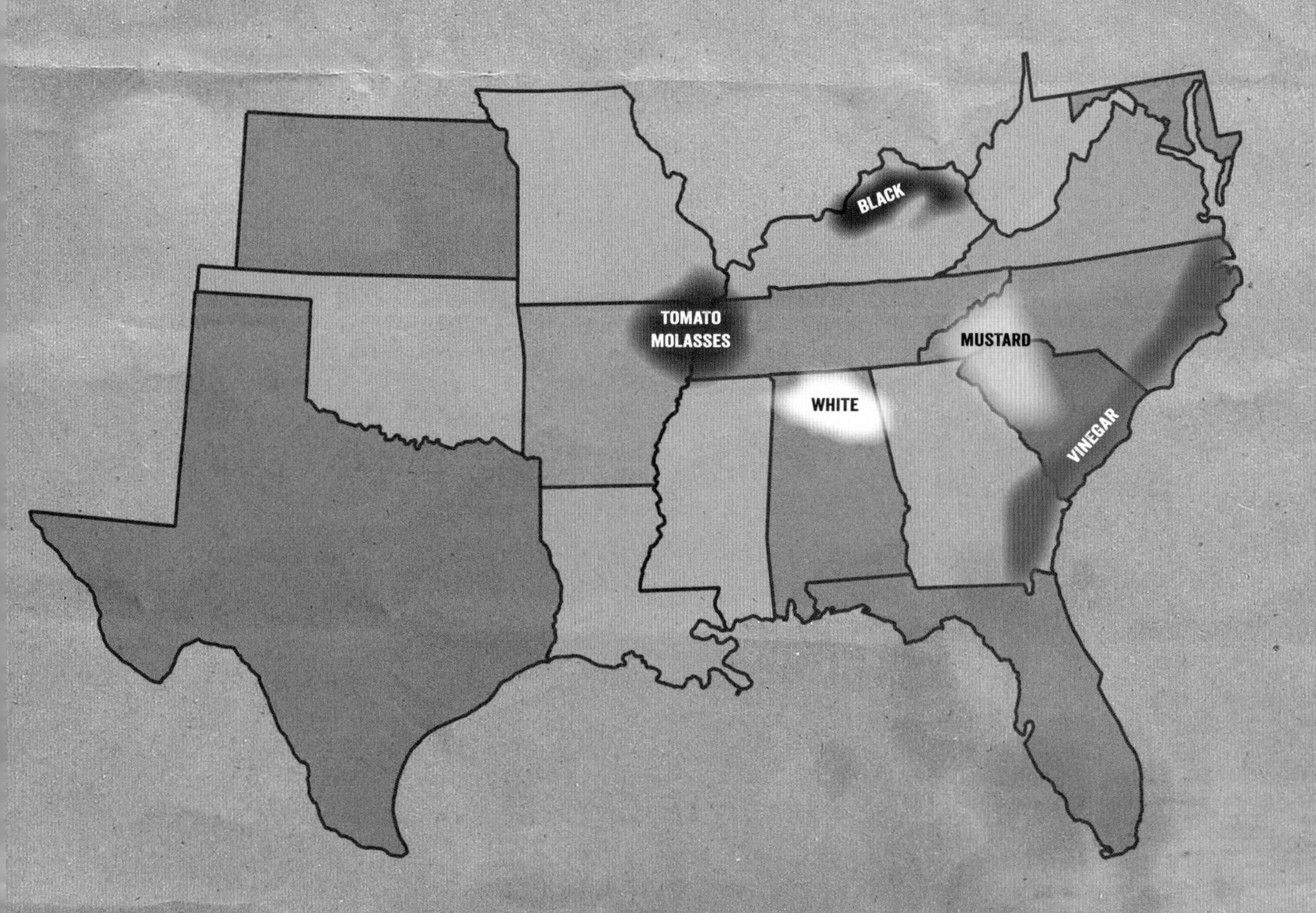

SWEET BBQ SAUCE

Close your eyes and imagine a backyard barbecue, and a plateful of ribs and all the trimmings just landed in your lap. Chances are all of that delicious meat was doused with a version of this sauce. Sticky, sweet, smoky . . . the ubiquitous condiment that works well with all types of barbecue fare.

MAKES ABOUT 3 CUPS • HANDS-ON: 5 MINUTES • TOTAL: 15 MINUTES

1 cup tomato paste or ketchup
1 cup (8 ounces) water
½ cup firmly packed light brown sugar
⅓ cup (about 3½ ounces) apple cider vinegar
1½ tablespoons molasses
1 tablespoon onion powder
1 tablespoon chili powder
1 tablespoon cracked black pepper
½ tablespoon garlic powder
2 teaspoons sea salt
1 teaspoon celery salt

Stir together all the ingredients in a medium saucepan, and bring to a boil over medium-high. Reduce heat to medium-low, and simmer until slightly thickened, about 10 minutes.

VINEGAR BBQ SAUCE

North Carolina is a state that has the battle lines firmly drawn when it comes to barbecue, not to mention barbecue sauces. If you were in eastern North Carolina, this sauce would be almost translucent (void of all tomatoes) and accompany a whole hog feast. If you found yourself in western North Carolina, your pork shoulder would arrive with a ruby red sauce that packs a vinegar punch. We've combined the best of both worlds for a veritable North Carolina "finishing sauce" that pairs well with pulled or chopped pork.

MAKES ABOUT 1½ CUPS • HANDS-ON: 5 MINUTES • TOTAL: 1 HOUR, 5 MINUTES

¾ cup (6 ounces) apple cider vinegar
½ cup tomato paste or ketchup
1½ tablespoons light brown sugar
1 tablespoon fresh lemon juice
1 teaspoon sea salt
1 teaspoon cayenne pepper
½ teaspoon cracked black pepper

Stir together all the ingredients in a small bowl; cover and chill 1 hour.

BLACK BBQ SAUCE

This regional western Kentucky sauce was created specifically to complement lamb or slow-smoked mutton. (Under 1 year = lamb, 1+ years = mutton, if we're scoring at home.) Much like the Vinegar BBQ Sauce (page 30), the Black BBQ Sauce is thin and perfectly penetrates the gamey taste of the mutton with notes of Worcestershire and vinegar on the nose. It sounds a little funky, but one taste and you'll understand why this tradition keeps getting passed down. It's a true taste of Appalachia.

MAKES ABOUT 3 CUPS • HANDS-ON: 5 MINUTES • TOTAL: 30 MINUTES

2 cups (16 ounces) water
½ cup firmly packed light brown sugar
½ cup (4 ounces) Worcestershire sauce
½ cup (4 ounces) apple cider vinegar
1 teaspoon fresh lemon juice
1 teaspoon sea salt
½ teaspoon garlic powder
½ teaspoon onion powder
½ teaspoon white pepper
½ teaspoon cracked black pepper
½ teaspoon ground allspice

Stir together all the ingredients in a medium saucepan; bring to a boil over medium, and simmer 15 minutes.

WHITE BBQ SAUCE

North Alabama claims this sauce, which pairs perfectly with smoked chicken and turkey. For a spicy variation, add ½ teaspoon of prepared horseradish (we prefer Atomic Horseradish) to complement brisket or pot roast. Don't shy away from substituting it in chicken/potato/shrimp salad for traditional mayo.

MAKES ABOUT 1 CUP • HANDS-ON: 5 MINUTES • TOTAL: 1 HOUR, 5 MINUTES

½ cup mayonnaise (such as Duke's)
2 tablespoons water
2 tablespoons apple cider vinegar
1 tablespoon light brown sugar
1 teaspoon fresh lemon juice
1 teaspoon cracked black pepper
½ teaspoon sea salt
½ teaspoon garlic powder
¼ teaspoon cayenne pepper

Stir together all the ingredients in a small bowl; cover and chill 1 hour.

MUSTARD BBQ SAUCE

From the coastal lowlands of South Carolina and southern Georgia, mustard reigns supreme. The mustard and vinegar bite is mellowed out with sweet honey and punched up with an added kick from three types of pepper. You definitely should try this versatile sauce in your next batch of coleslaw or potato salad—or even as a dipping sauce for crispy French fries or onion rings. Serve warm over pulled pork, chicken, pork chops, sausage, or brisket.

MAKES ABOUT 2¾ CUPS • HANDS-ON: 5 MINUTES • TOTAL: 8 MINUTES, PLUS CHILLING TIME

1½ cups yellow mustard
½ cup apple cider vinegar
½ cup honey
1 tablespoon light brown sugar
1 tablespoon tomato paste or ketchup
1 teaspoon cracked black pepper
1 teaspoon white pepper
½ teaspoon sea salt
½ teaspoon garlic powder
½ teaspoon cayenne pepper

Stir together all the ingredients in a small bowl. Chill 8 hours or overnight for the best flavor. Transfer to a medium saucepan, and cook over medium-low, stirring often, until heated through, about 5 minutes. (Do not boil.)

SMOKEHOUSE STORIES AND RECIPES

with
TECHRON
Gasoline
Self Serve
Unleaded
Diesel
BBQ
BUTTS TO GO
CHICKEN • RIBS • WINGS & MORE!

BUTTS TO GO ♦ PELL CITY, ALABAMA

"I KEPT SEEING TELEVISION SPOTS WITH CINDY CRAWFORD EVERY FIFTEEN MINUTES ADVERTISING ROOMS TO GO, SO I THOUGHT, WHY NOT HAVE SOME FUN, AND NAME OUR LITTLE JOINT BUTTS TO GO?" THAT'S THE PROMOTIONAL AND HUMOROUS WORKINGS COMING FROM THE MIND OF PITMASTER WADE REICH IN PELL CITY, ALABAMA. SITUATED INSIDE A TEXACO SERVICE STATION, IT'S JUST ONE OF MANY LINES I LEARN FROM WADE—AND I SOON FIND OUT THAT HIS SAVVY PROMOTIONAL AWARENESS STRETCHES FAR BEYOND THE BYWAYS OF I-20.

Born and raised in Gadsden, Alabama, Reich was born into the hospitality business. His great grandfather, David Reich, a merchant-turned-hotelier, was responsible for owning and running the Printup Hotel until he died in 1914. His grandfather, Adolph Philip Reich, "Poppo," took over the business of operating the cherished hotel, while also building the Reich Hotel, among several others, throughout his career. Their establishments once served as the crown jewels of Gadsden—inviting travelers, congressmen, and dignitaries from all over the country to bask in their gilded era glow.

Wade got an early start in the business by way of loading the hotel freight elevators to refill the Coca-Cola machines in the hotel. His second job was in the kitchen, working alongside (aka washing dishes) chef Emile Sevin. His third job was bagging groceries at the Piggly Wiggly. In case you can't tell, he's sort of a jack-of-all-trades, master of many, type of guy.

Wade attended the University of Alabama (wait for it . . . Roll Tide) and got a degree in marketing. After graduation, he returned to his Gadsden roots to remodel the lobby of the Printup, creating his own restaurant when the town finally went from dry to wet. "Poppos," the name of the eatery and a family nickname, was his way of honoring the family patriarchs and legacy of hospitality. You see, Wade credits his father, Bobby, for teaching him the way around the kitchen—that know-how combined with a mix of Southern and Creole cooking shows.

Then there's the second phase of Wade's career, a phase that played well into his promotional and marketing expertise. A chance meeting with businessman Dan Wallace set up by Mary Hardin in Birmingham led Wade into the supermarket promotion business. Long before the SkyMiles-esque loyalty programs of today, supermarkets would reward housewives who shopped at their establishments during certain periods of time with free dishware, for example, for their loyalty. Such promotions were a hit with stores and consumers alike—and not just in the state of Alabama.

Wade spent nearly two decades dividing his time between homes in London and Paris, running such promotions throughout Europe.

After returning to the states, Tim Jackson, a friend, invited Wade to go in on a local service station. He smiles and laughs, "wondering why Tim even invited him into the business in the first place." A few years later, they acquired the Texaco in which we currently stand. So what about the BBQ? Well, in all his Southern

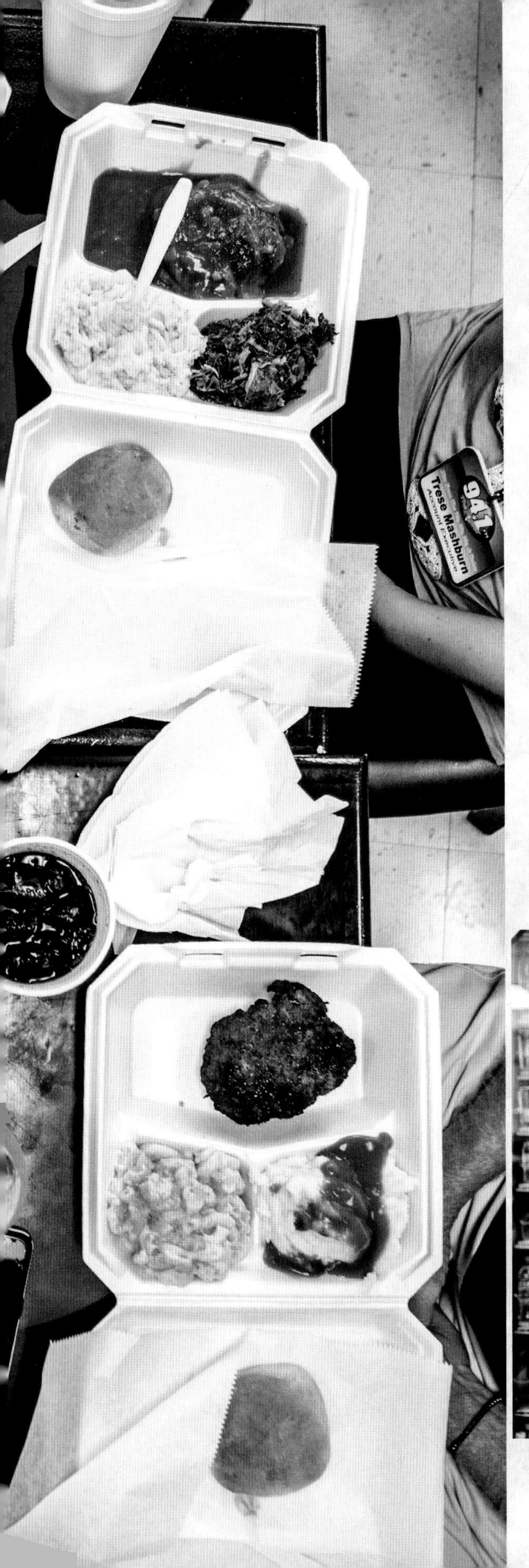

gentleman charm, Wade tells me that, "The gas business got so bad that it made the food business look good."

He perfected his method of BBQ through trial and error. Over the years, he has learned to hone his craft, while maintaining precise consistency. Wade tells me, "An inconsistent restaurant will shutter prior to one that serves bad food consistently." I have to agree.

This place serves as a quick in-and-out eatery for families and hungry road warriors to literally get their butts to go. Within an off-hour on a weekday, I notice at least a dozen or so folks coming in and requesting their previously placed order for a smoked butt. Others are scattered about the convenience store digging into their food.

I can't imagine a more unpretentious environment for such a well-traveled, humble, and honestly cool cat to serve such delicious food. It's entirely fitting.

Perhaps true to form, or true to fate, I gas up and pack up a butt all on-site for the short haul back to Music City. I burst into laughter when I see my first Rooms To Go billboard.

That's the good stuff, I'll tell ya.

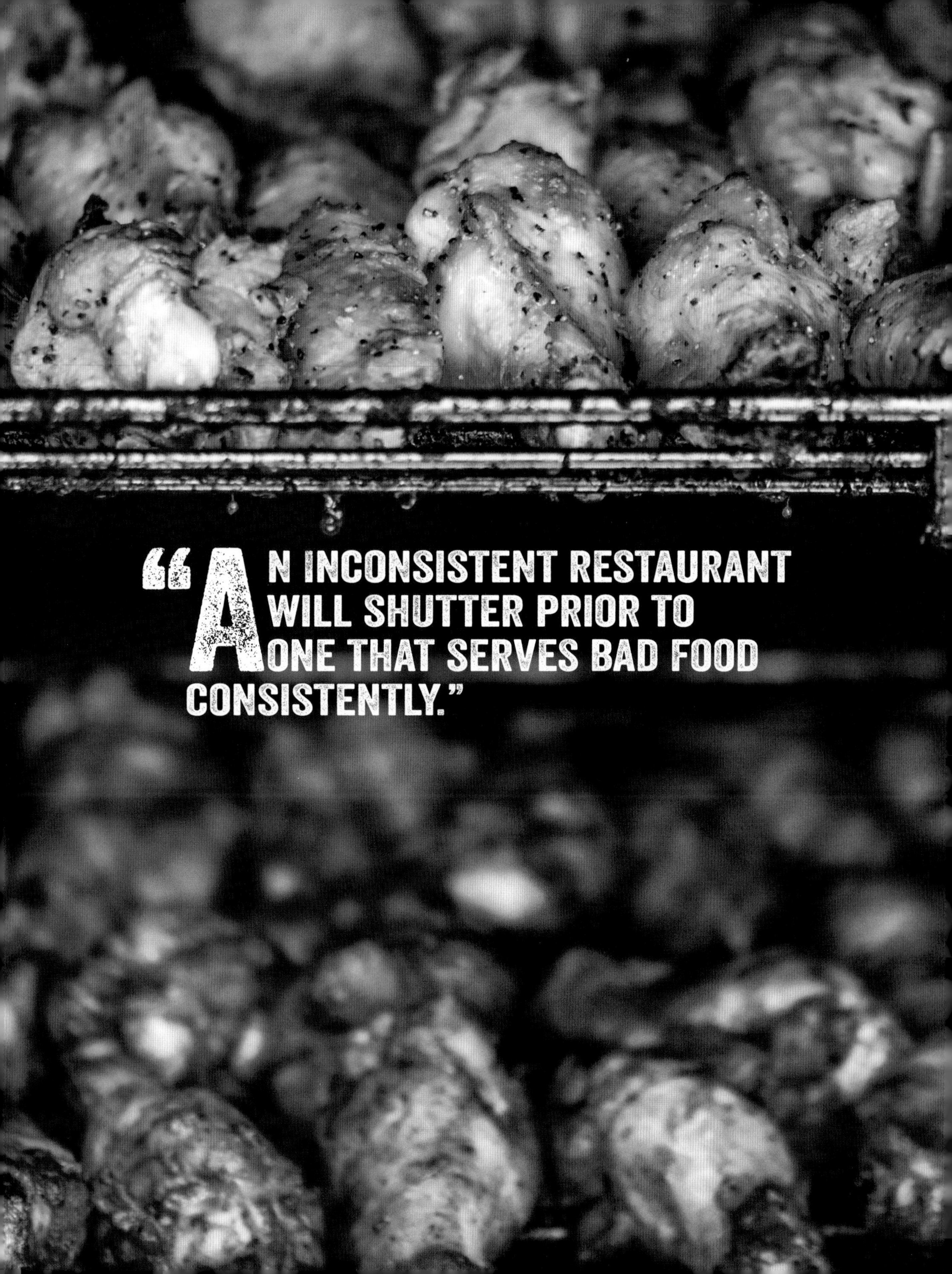
"AN INCONSISTENT RESTAURANT WILL SHUTTER PRIOR TO ONE THAT SERVES BAD FOOD CONSISTENTLY."

BUTTS TO GO PORK BUTT

Some call it sacrilegious to use Liquid Smoke—sure, I know what you are thinking. Here's the deal—Wade doesn't care. He uses the concoction to allow his steakhouse-style rub to stick to the meat. The real flavor comes from hard-earned hickory smoke, which is heavily infused during a two-hour smoking process. From there, Wade tells me he relies on the ol' "Texas crutch" method, wrapping the butt in foil until it's tender like butter. He tests the butts by poking them with a dulled thermometer point to ensure they reach his desired texture. From there he sells the butts to go or pulls the meat and serves it on top of a basic bun with a "middle-of-the-road" commercial sauce he chose for its balanced tang and sweetness that suits many tastes. Let me tell you something—there ain't nothing middle of the road about his pork!

SERVES 10 • HANDS-ON: 15 MINUTES • TOTAL: 12 HOURS, 45 MINUTES, INCLUDING RUB

Hickory wood chunks
1 (8-pound) bone-in pork butt (Boston butt)
2 tablespoons Liquid Smoke
¼ cup Butts to Go Butt Rub (recipe below)
White hamburger buns, such as Sunbeam brand
Cattleman's BBQ Smoky Base Barbecue Sauce and pickle chips (optional)

1. Prepare smoker according to manufacturer's instructions with an area cleared of coals to create an indirect-heat area, bringing internal temperature to 230°F; maintain temperature 15 to 20 minutes. Place wood chunks on coals.
2. Rinse the pork, and pat dry. Rub the Liquid Smoke on pork until liberally coated; coat with butt rub.
3. Smoke the pork over indirect heat, maintaining temperature inside smoker around 230°F for 2 hours.
4. Remove the pork from smoker; wrap in aluminum foil. Return to smoker, and smoke over indirect heat until tender and a meat thermometer inserted in thickest portion registers 200°F, about 10 hours.
5. Remove the pork from smoker; remove and discard foil. Let stand 30 minutes. Remove and discard the bone and fat cap. Pull the pork by hand. Serve on the buns with sauce, if desired.

BUTTS TO GO BUTT RUB

2 tablespoons kosher salt
2 tablespoons freshly ground black pepper
2 tablespoons smoked paprika
1½ tablespoons granulated garlic
1 tablespoon granulated onion
1 tablespoon dried crushed coriander
1 tablespoon red pepper flakes

Stir together all the ingredients in a small bowl. Use immediately, or store in an airtight container up to 6 months to 1 year. Makes ⅔ cup

FLAKE
Nutrition
GINGER

ALE

DRY-RUBBED SMOKED CHICKEN WINGS

Butts ain't the only item highly demanded from Wade's clientele. His wings are equally delicious. They come on and off the smoker throughout the day just to keep up with demand. The low-and-slow method ensures that the meat remains super moist and fall-off-the-bone tender, with a deliciously melded skin that is heavily seasoned with an in-house rub. I'm beginning to think these wings might play a part in the success of Wade's alma mater on a game day.

SERVES 2 • HANDS-ON: 10 MINUTES • TOTAL: 1 HOUR, 40 MINUTES, INCLUDING RUB

1 pound chicken wings and drumettes
2 tablespoons Butts To Go Wing Rub (recipe below)

1. Prepare smoker according to manufacturer's instructions with an area cleared of coals to create an indirect-heat area, bringing internal temperature to 215°F; maintain temperature 15 to 20 minutes. Toss the wings and drumettes in wing rub until liberally coated.
2. Smoke the chicken over indirect heat, maintaining temperature inside smoker around 215°F until done, 1½ to 2 hours.

BUTTS TO GO WING RUB

Paprika, along with a good bit of salt, plays the dominant role in this fragrant, orange-hued rub. This rub works great with poultry items, like the smoked turkey on page 46. My advice? Don't be too shy about trying it out as a finishing seasoning for soft scrambled eggs.

½ cup paprika
¼ cup kosher salt
¼ cup freshly ground black pepper
¼ cup garlic powder
2½ tablespoons dried oregano
2 tablespoons cayenne pepper

Stir together all the ingredients in a small bowl. Use immediately, or store in an airtight container up to 6 months to 1 year. Makes about 2 cups

WADE'S BAKED BEANS

A good bit of the pulled pork helps to tie together this simple recipe, along with some favorite condiments. The real kicker, however, is the actual smoke that the beans take on while reaching their bubbly delicious state on the smoker.

SERVES 10 • HANDS-ON: 10 MINUTES • TOTAL: 1 HOUR, 30 MINUTES

4 (16.5-ounce) cans baked beans
½ pound pulled pork
½ cup ketchup
½ cup Cattleman's BBQ Smoky Base Barbecue Sauce
¼ cup yellow mustard

1. Prepare smoker according to manufacturer's instructions with an area cleared of coals to create an indirect-heat area, bringing internal temperature to 250°F; maintain temperature 15 to 20 minutes. Combine all the ingredients in a 13- x 9-inch aluminum foil disposable pan, and cover with aluminum foil.
2. Place foil pan on smoker over indirect heat; smoke 1 hour, maintaining temperature inside smoker around 250°F. Uncover and smoke until mixture is reduced and bubbly, about 20 minutes. Serve immediately.

SMOKED TURKEY SANDWICH

Smoking turkey ain't easy. Wade keeps it super moist by injecting the breast with butter (duh!).

SERVES 8 TO 10 • HANDS-ON: 10 MINUTES • TOTAL: 2 HOURS, 40 MINUTES

Hickory wood chips
4 ounces (½ cup) unsalted butter, melted
1 (10-pound) skin-on, boneless turkey breast
¼ cup Butts To Go Wing Rub (page 45)
Thick-cut white bread, toasted
Bottled spicy Ranch dressing
Thick-cut hickory-smoked bacon slices, cooked
Tomato slices
Iceberg lettuce

1. Prepare smoker according to manufacturer's instructions with an area cleared of coals to create an indirect-heat area. Place hickory wood chips on coals, and bring internal temperature to 265°F; maintain temperature 15 to 20 minutes. Meanwhile, using a syringe, inject the melted butter throughout turkey breast. Pat the turkey dry, and coat in wing rub.
2. Smoke the turkey over indirect heat, maintaining temperature inside smoker around 265°F until a meat thermometer inserted in thickest portion registers 165°F, about 2 hours. Remove the turkey from smoker. Tent with foil, and let stand 30 minutes.
3. Slice the turkey breast. Layer the sliced turkey on toasted bread smeared with dressing. Top with the bacon, tomato, and lettuce.

Katy + Mikie
Houston TX
WORD STREET
APRIL 30 2008
e Sausage-Maker's Daughter
Walls honors her father's legacy by opening Johnson's Boucaniere. By Mary Tutwiler
Briguy - Fieri
approved.
Good stuff
AWESOME!!
FROM NOLA
CANADIANS.
Three years ago, Wallace Johnson,
son of Johnson's Grocery owner Arneastor
Johnson, thought the store's 2005 closing was
an end of an era. "A lot of the customers we
built on were friends," he said. "A lot of them
floor, the door was sealed, and the meat
smoked for hours. On a clear day with
little humidity, the smoked meat came
out deep, succulent red. Customers came
for some sausage for their beans or sauce
piquant and usually left with a link of
Johnson's signature boudin, a warm baked
sweet potato from the basket near the register, and if they were lucky, a cup of the
hand-dripped strong coffee the Johnson
brothers drank in the morning.
Lori has tripled the size of the smoking
operation here in Lafayette. Her smokehouse has four compartments, each with its
The Food Produc
here are
great !!!

HOT
BOUDIN
TO-DAY
TM

JOHNSON'S
BOUCANIERE
YETI
SUN
THE LEGENDARY SUN STUDIO
RAGIN' CAJUNS
REVE

JOHNSON'S BOUCANIÈRE • LAFAYETTE, LOUISIANA

ONE THING IS CERTAIN ABOUT THE BBQ AT JOHNSON'S BOUCANIÈRE . . . IT'S ALL ABOUT FAMILY. I'M STANDING IN THE RESTAURANT, DESIGNED BY OWNER GREG WALLS (HE'S ALSO AN ARCHITECT) AND SPEAKING TO HIS FATHER-IN-LAW, WALLACE JOHNSON, ABOUT THE PRIDE OF SEEING HIS DAUGHTER LORI AND SON-IN-LAW GREG CARRYING ON THIS FAMILY TRADITION. NEARLY 90 YEARS OLD, WALLACE IS WALKING ME BEHIND THE VINTAGE REGISTER DESCRIBING OLD PHOTOS WITH EXACTING DETAIL, WHILE ALSO SHOWCASING HIS PAINTINGS THAT ADORN THE WALLS. PERHAPS HIS MOST FAMOUS, WRITTEN ON WHITE AND ETCHED IN RED ARE THE WORDS "HOT BOUDIN TO-DAY!"

When pressed on the unusual spelling, he simply tells me, "It's just the way I did it back then but 'To-Day' it's, you know, sort of like my signature."

Signature indeed. Johnson's Boucanière is carrying on a family tradition that dates back to 1937. Founded in Eunice, Louisiana, by Arneastor Johnson, Johnson's Grocery long served as a staple of the community, occupying three locations on Maple Drive until it closed in 2005. Wallace, Lori's father, continued his father's tradition of running the store, with a focus on dry goods and meat. In fact, to their knowledge, Johnson's Grocery was the first establishment in Louisiana permitted to commercially sell meat. Not just any meat. It's all about the boudin—a ground pork and rice mixture filled with the Cajun trinity and seasonings and stuffed into casings. During that era, the Johnson family—parents, kids, cousins, and all—would make up to 2,000 pounds of boudin every Saturday just to satisfy the community.

After the grocery closed in 2005, Lori longed for the boudin and sausages she grew up eating. Ever the innovator, her husband, Greg, rigged up the family fireplace so they could experiment smoking their own sausages. It was either luck or destiny, when moving the old mixer out of the old store caused them to find a trove of the old family recipes for tasso, jerky, and sausage. The way Greg tells it, the mixer was too large to fit through the door, so when they removed the door, they found the old recipes on the backside just waiting to be rediscovered.

In 2008, the couple opened Johnson's Boucanière in Lafayette, Louisiana. Lori admits that opening was beyond stressful, noting a huge responsibility to carry on the family tradition. "Beyond high quality food and consistency, I want everyone who walks in to feel at home, cared for, and important," says Lori. Greg, born and raised in Bloomington, Indiana, knew that he wanted to expand beyond the original grocery concept so he took his passion for BBQ and placed it front and center. "Louisiana rightfully has so much other great food that BBQ is not typically associated with our state. I took my upbringing and experience, combined with the tradition of Lori's family, to create our own unique style," says Greg. Johnson's is, without a doubt, unique. I'm devouring pulled pork, sliced brisket, and boneless ribs right alongside boudin, gumbo, and whatever specialty Lori serves up as a "plate lunch" for the day.

Admittedly, I'm not exactly sure what Lori means by the term "plate lunch"—something that was a staple at the grocery and known by most Louisianans. Essentially, she tells me it's a special of the day, consisting of a meat option and two sides. Later in our conversation she tells me that customers also expect, without exception, a side of rice and gravy too! Me being the Nashville guy, I think of it as a meat and three. Call it what you will. I call it delicious—especially her Sausage and Tasso Sauce Piquant.

It's not just the variety of fare that allows Johnson's to stand apart—it's also its preparation. Greg's architectural expertise really shines when you walk to the back of the house to examine his masterpiece—a closed pit he custom-built, using live oak both as a heat source and for smoke.

I've never seen anything like it—and just one piece of tasso coming fresh off the smoker and straight into my mouth makes me a believer. I keep eating whatever he gives me—eyeing the meats coming off the smoker like a kid in Willy Wonka's chocolate factory.

If Lori and Greg had doubts about carrying on the family tradition, I can say it is alive and well in Lafayette, Louisiana. Go get yourself a plate lunch with some boudin, 'cue, and all the fixin's. It's hot, served with love, and ready To-Day!

“IT’S JUST THE WAY I DID IT BACK THEN BUT ‘TO-DAY’ IT’S, YOU KNOW, SORT OF LIKE MY SIGNATURE.”

RAGIN
CAJUNS
JOHNSON'S
BOUCANIÈRE
LAFAYETTE, LOUISIANA
Fisher-Price

Stevie's Stuffed Grilled Cheese

JOHNSON'S BOUCANIÈRE PORK BUTT

Greg's custom smokers impart the most smoke flavor in the first six or seven hours. From there, he places the butts in shallow tins with some water, covers them with foil, and places the "tin-ed" butts back on the smoker for an additional seven to eight hours. The result is some of most tender and juicy pork I have ever tried.

SERVES 10 TO 12 • HANDS-ON: 15 MINUTES • TOTAL: 12 HOURS, 15 MINUTES

1 (8- to 10-pound) bone-in pork butt (Boston butt)
¼ cup Greg's Dry Rub (page 61)
Oak charcoal
1½ cups (12 ounces) water

1. Rinse the pork thoroughly, and trim away any bone chips or cartilage. Pat the pork dry, and season liberally with dry rub. Store in the refrigerator for 24 hours.
2. Prepare smoker according to manufacturer's instructions, using oak wood embers, bringing internal temperature to 250°F to 275°F; maintain temperature 15 to 20 minutes.
3. Smoke the pork, covered, maintaining temperature between 250°F to 275°F, for 7 hours or until a meat thermometer inserted in thickest portion registers 200°F. Remove the pork, and place in a 13- x 9-inch lasagna-style aluminum foil pan. Add 1½ cups water to the pan (do not pour over the top), cover with foil, and return to the smoker for 5 to 6 more hours or until the bone pulls cleanly from the pork butt. Remove the fat cap and bone, and pull by hand. Serve immediately.

STEVIE'S STUFFED GRILLED CHEESE

Lori credits her niece Stevie Rauls for this ridiculously good concoction. Since Johnson's sits between two schools, they wanted to add something to the menu that was kid-friendly.

SERVES 1 • HANDS-ON: 10 MINUTES • TOTAL: 10 MINUTES

1 tablespoon unsalted butter
1 white hamburger bun, split
2 American cheese slices
4 ounces pulled pork

Melt the butter in a cast-iron pan or on a griddle over medium. Place the bun halves, cut side up, in butter. Place 1 cheese slice on each bun half. Top the bottom bun half with the pulled pork. Using a spatula, place the top bun half, cheese side down, on pulled pork. Cook, turning occasionally and gently pressing with spatula, until the cheese is melted, about 5 minutes. Serve immediately.

SAUSAGE AND TASSO SAUCE PIQUANT

This Cajun classic is one of the most popular offerings on the plate lunch menu. Tasso is a heavily smoked and salted piece of ham that is widely used in Cajun cooking. You can find it in specialty stores and online. Unfortunately, it ain't so easy with Johnson's Cajun pork sausage. You'll need to make a visit (which is entirely worth it!) in order to get their sausage. That said, Greg and Lori tell me that any Cajun smoked pork sausage will work just fine.

SERVES 8 • HANDS-ON: 20 MINUTES • TOTAL: 2 HOURS, 25 MINUTES

1 pound Cajun smoked pork sausage, cut into ¼-inch slices
½ pound tasso (Cajun smoked ham), diced
2 tablespoons unsalted butter
1 sweet onion, diced
½ green bell pepper, diced
2 celery stalks, diced
2 garlic cloves, minced
1¼ cups canned diced tomatoes and green chiles (such as Rotel)
1 cup tomato sauce
1 cup (8 ounces) water
1 teaspoon Creole seasoning
Hot cooked rice
Sliced scallions

1. Cook the sausage and tasso in a Dutch oven over medium-high, stirring occasionally, until heated through, about 5 minutes. Using a slotted spoon, transfer the sausage and tasso to a plate, reserving drippings in Dutch oven.

2. Reduce heat to medium, and melt the butter in Dutch oven. Add the onion, bell pepper, celery, and garlic, and cook, stirring often, until vegetables are just tender, 5 to 7 minutes. Stir in the diced tomatoes and chiles, tomato sauce, water, Creole seasoning, and sausage and tasso. Cover and reduce heat to medium-low. Cook, stirring occasionally, until the sauce has thickened, about 1 hour and 30 minutes. For a thicker sauce, uncover during last 30 minutes of cooking.

3. Serve over the hot cooked rice. Top with the scallion slices.

6.25
6.00
5.75

HOT
BOUDIN
TO-DAY

round to
porch
BUY LEAUXCAL
Johnson's Boucaniere
ICE COLD
PREMIUM SUGARCANE SODA
SWAMP POP
ROOT BEER

4oz
8oz
12oz
16oz
theres a party in my tummy!!
So yummy
LONG LIVE THE NÉNAINE
7AM-10AM
Nénaine
biscuit
Stuffed
Your choice
2 slices
Pulled Pork:
Build Your
Start with
Pulled Pork: $3.25
Sausage: $3.25
Boudin: $3.25
Boucanière
Includes a biscuit
Add-ons:
Pulled pork:
Sausage: $2.00
Brisket:
SIDES
BBQ Tots:
Grits: $1.25
Fruit

BBQ TOTS

Do not let the name fool you. These are more hash brown than tots, and they are a customer favorite every day of the week. Like most good things in life, these potato nuggets were a happy accident. A cook working the griddle mistakenly used the BBQ rub instead of the normal seasoning. Instead of remaking the batch, Lori suggested they give 'em a try. They've been made in the same mistaken manner ever since!

SERVES 6 • HANDS-ON: 25 MINUTES • TOTAL: 25 MINUTES, INCLUDING RUB

2 ounces (¼ cup) unsalted butter
½ sweet onion, cut into ½-inch pieces
½ green bell pepper, cut into ½-inch pieces
4 baked potatoes, cut into 1-inch pieces
2 tablespoons Greg's Dry Rub (recipe below)

Melt the butter in a large cast-iron skillet over medium-high. Add the onion and bell pepper; cook, stirring often, until tender, 3 to 4 minutes. Add the potatoes and dry rub, making sure potatoes are in contact with the bottom of the skillet. Cook, without stirring, 8 minutes. Using a spatula, flip the mixture, and cook until browned, about 8 more minutes.

GREG'S DRY RUB

The exact recipe for this rub is held under lock and key, but Greg was kind enough to share the ingredients so I could engineer my own version. This rub is less Creole than I had originally imagined. It's salty and sweet with a nice backbone of heat but not as aromatic as most Creole seasonings. The smoky essence of chili powder along with the tanginess of dry mustard balances the fatty flavor of the pork.

1 cup loosely packed light brown sugar
2½ tablespoons paprika
2 tablespoons kosher salt
1 tablespoon freshly ground black pepper
1 tablespoon red pepper flakes
1 tablespoon chili powder
1 tablespoon onion powder
1 tablespoon garlic powder
1 tablespoon dry mustard

Stir together all the ingredients in a small bowl. Use immediately, or store in an airtight container up to 6 months to 1 year. Makes 1¾ cups

1627
BOGART'S
SMOKE HOUSE
HOURS
Mon - Thur
10:30 ~ 4ish
(or until we get tired)
Fri - Sat
10:30 ~
Skip Steele
Executive Chef

BOGART'S SMOKEHOUSE • ST. LOUIS, MISSOURI

"COOKING IS A MATH PROBLEM: TIME + TEMPERATURE = RESULTS." THAT SIMPLE STATEMENT MIGHT BE THE MOST IMPORTANT PIECE OF INFORMATION THAT I GLEANED FROM PITMASTER SKIP STEELE. AS THE LINE STARTS TO BUILD OUTSIDE OF BOGART'S SMOKEHOUSE IN ST. LOUIS'S SOULARD NEIGHBORHOOD, SKIP REMINDS ME OF THAT EQUATION TIME AND AGAIN AS HE PULLS OFF SMOKED WINGS, RIBS, TRI-TIP, BRISKET, PASTRAMI, BURNT ENDS, AND, OF COURSE, PORK BUTT FROM THE SMOKER. I CAN'T EVEN WAIT FOR THE MEAT TO COOL DOWN—BURNING MY FINGERTIPS AND TONGUE AS I SAMPLE EVERY BIT OF SKIP'S MASTERY.

I use my own equation, however, to describe Skip's barbecue: Experience + Simplicity + Humility = Damn Good 'Cue.

With nearly 40 years of barbecuing under his belt, experience is something that Skip isn't short on. Born and raised outside of Memphis, Skip grew up as a farm boy, learning how to cook at 12 years old in his grandfather's kitchen. At 13, he started working for a gentleman who owned a junkyard. Seeing a pile of unused propane tanks one day, the owner of the junkyard told Skip they were all his—so long as he was careful. Using his "farm boy" welding skills, something he still utilizes today, Skip built his first smoker from the scrap metal. I like to think that most good small businesses start out of necessity. So, when a gentleman pulled up into Skip's front yard and asked for a smoker, Skip sold him the one he had just made. Soon afterward, throughout his teens, he built more custom smokers and grills, catering to any customer's request.

During this point in our conversation, I start to realize that Skip is not only a mighty fine pitmaster, but he might also be the most interesting man in the world, seriously. An academic scholarship, participation on the rifle team, and a full-time job working as a grain operator for the USDA didn't entirely satisfy Skip while he attended Arkansas State University in Jonesboro, Arkansas. So, when a fraternity brother bought a convenience store in town, Skip asked to place a smoker out front. He tells me that soon there was a three-week waiting list for one of his smoked chickens. If you weren't there to pick it up by 5 p.m., there'd be a line of folks just salivating to take your perfectly cooked, juicy bird.

With my meat coma setting in, I'm finally understanding that it's not only Skip's experience behind the grill but also his travels that play a huge part in his knowledge of what it takes to make perfection. After a stint working on the Mexican border, Skip, now married, was encouraged, he says with a laugh, by his wife to get a "real job." He went on to garner a captain's rank as a Marine Surveyor—working (and, of course, eating) in ports all over the world.

Upon retirement in his mid-forties, the same wife, he tells me with another laugh, asked what was next. Skip knew exactly what to do—return to his roots. A stint in Manhattan and Las Vegas as an executive chef sparked what would become his hallowed ground of barbecue in St. Louis—a town known for authentic 'cue. He started out by opening Pappy's, which required expansion upon expansion to accommodate serving nearly 2,000 customers a day.

But it's Bogart's Smokehouse that serves as Skip's crown jewel—he casually refers to it as his "test kitchen." Bogart's is the kind of place where he practices his hybrid form of barbecue—encompassing all of his knowledge and literally welding it all together. At any joint, one can expect perfectly cooked pork butt, ribs, chicken, and brisket. Then there's Skip's hoisin-marinated tri-tip, which pays homage to Asia and Southern California, while his house-cured pastrami harkens back to experiences in New York and Montreal. He uses that welding

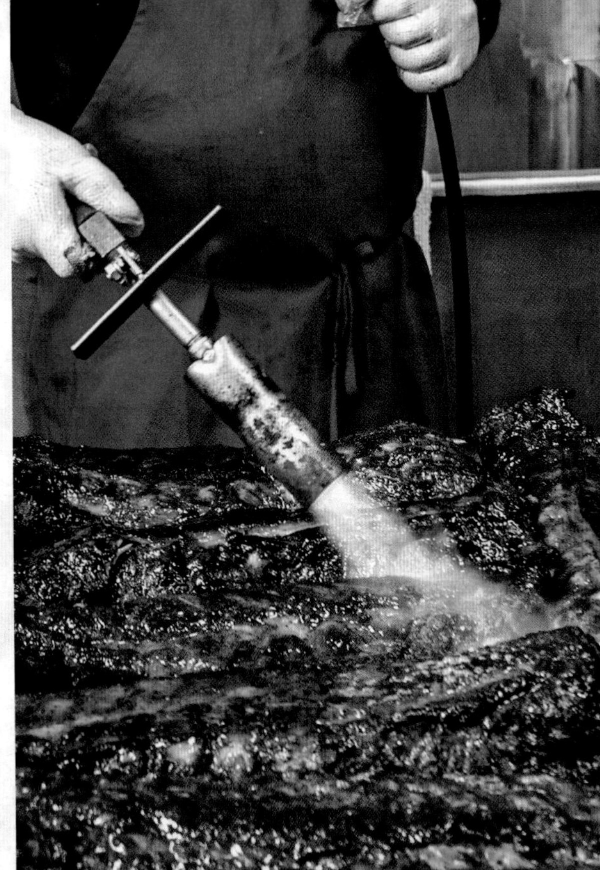

knowledge when he pulls out a blowtorch to caramelize an apricot glaze on his ribs—enough said. It's these "test" items, along with the perfected classics like the 20-hour pork butt, which really shine. Turns out, what Skip humbly refers to as his test kitchen is actually a top-rated barbecue restaurant in America as the constant line out the door for several city blocks proves.

A stout man, built much like a defensive lineman, Skip sports his chef's camo pants as he greets everyone who comes in the door—often handing out snacks to those waiting in 2+ hour line. The way he sees it, "There are a bunch of places to get a pork sandwich, and if nobody talks to you, it's just a pork sandwich." So it's not just the great food, but it's also the humble service and attention to detail that keeps the customers coming back day after day.

Cheers to you, Captain.

Single Serve
Pepper
Contains: Ground Black Pepper.
DIAMOND CRYSTAL BRANDS, INC.
SAVANNAH, GA 31405
BOGART'S
SMOKE HOUSE

BOGART'S PORK BUTT

The key to perfecting this deliciously tender butt is all about keeping it very low and very slow. The constant 200°F smoke for 20 hours will yield a butt that can literally be pulled apart by hand. Serve it Bogart's style atop a brioche bun with sauce on the side—or simply serve on its own. The wild cherry smoke and 24-hour marinade provide enough flavor to complement the delicious pork, while never overpowering.

SERVES 10 • HANDS-ON: 20 MINUTES
TOTAL: 21 HOURS, 20 MINUTES, INCLUDING RUB, SMOKING, PLUS 1 DAY CHILLING TIME

1 (8- to 10-pound) bone-in pork butt (Boston butt)
1 cup yellow mustard
½ cup Old-School Butt Rub (recipe below)
Wild cherry wood chunks

1. Rinse the pork thoroughly with cold water, and pat dry. Score fat on the pork butt in a crisscross pattern about 1 inch apart.
2. Coat the pork in a thin, even layer of mustard. Liberally sprinkle with butt rub. Loosely cover, and chill 24 hours.
3. Prepare smoker according to manufacturer's instructions with an area cleared of coals to create an indirect-heat area, bringing internal temperature to 200°F; maintain temperature 15 to 20 minutes. Place wild cherry wood chunks on coals.
4. Smoke the pork over indirect heat, maintaining temperature inside smoker around 200°F and adding more charcoal, if necessary, until a meat thermometer inserted in thickest portion registers 200°F, about 20 hours.
5. Remove the pork from smoker. Wrap in aluminum foil, and wrap in plastic wrap. Let stand 1 hour. (If serving later, wrap in towels, and place in a cooler until ready to serve.)
6. Using your hands, remove the fatty layer and bone from pork. Gently pull the meat, and serve immediately.

OLD-SCHOOL BUTT RUB

Sweet and savory, with plenty of aromatics, this all-purpose rub provides the perfect seasoning for any pork butt. Be sure to season the butt liberally, ensuring an even coating of seasonings over the butt.

2 tablespoons granulated sugar
2 tablespoons kosher salt
2 teaspoons hot smoked paprika
1 teaspoon freshly ground black pepper
1 teaspoon chili powder
1 teaspoon red pepper flakes
1 teaspoon ground allspice
1 teaspoon ground nutmeg
½ teaspoon MSG (monosodium glutamate)

Stir together all the ingredients in a bowl, and store in an airtight container up to 1 year. Makes ½ cup

FIRE AND ICE PICKLES

Sweet, tangy, and with a touch of heat, these almost-candied pickles are super addictive. In fact, they are often a requested side dish at Bogart's. Skip came up with the idea nearly two decades ago when visiting a restaurant in Mississippi. He carried a shipman's journal everywhere he ate, and when Bogart's opened, he searched back into his archive to perfect this pickle that serves as a customer favorite today.

MAKES 1 QUART • HANDS-ON: 10 MINUTES • TOTAL: 10 MINUTES, PLUS 3 DAYS CHILLING TIME

1 quart dill pickle chips
¾ cup granulated sugar
¼ cup hot sauce (such as Frank's Red Hot)
1 tablespoon minced garlic
1 teaspoon cayenne pepper

1. Reserve 1 cup of the pickle juice from pickle jar. Place the pickles in a colander; drain and rinse with cold running water 3 times.
2. Stir together the sugar, hot sauce, garlic, cayenne pepper, and reserved pickle juice. Return the pickles to pickle jar; pour sugar mixture over pickles. Cover and chill 3 days before serving.

BROWN SUGAR AND BALSAMIC

This simple sauce, crafted by Skip, really blew my mind in terms of complexity and simplicity. He claims that he has a very "middle-of-the-road" palate, meaning that if he likes it, most folks like it. If he doesn't, well, you get the idea. A great pitmaster must first understand and master the use of salt and pepper. After that, it's about acid and sugar. This sauce showcases the latter—proving that just two ingredients can provide a complex sauce that's great on any smoked meat.

MAKES ABOUT 1 CUP • HANDS-ON: 5 MINUTES • TOTAL: 5 MINUTES

2 cups firmly packed light brown sugar
¾ cup (6 ounces) balsamic vinegar

Combine the sugar and vinegar in a small heavy-bottomed saucepan over medium. Cook, whisking constantly, until sugar is dissolved. Bring to a low simmer, whisking constantly. Remove from heat. Cool and serve with smoked meat.

MAD MADDIE

This is an Eastern Carolina-style sauce that packs plenty of tang and acidity, while also packing some peppery heat. Mop it on pork butt, ribs, and smoked chicken. It also works as a great marinade or finishing sauce.

MAKES ABOUT 1½ CUPS • HANDS-ON: 5 MINUTES • TOTAL: 5 MINUTES

1½ cups (12 ounces) white wine vinegar
1 tablespoon cayenne pepper
1 tablespoon paprika
1 tablespoon kosher salt

Combine all the ingredients in a clean glass jar with a lid. Cover and shake vigorously until solids have dissolved. Serve immediately with the pork butt, ribs, or smoked chicken.

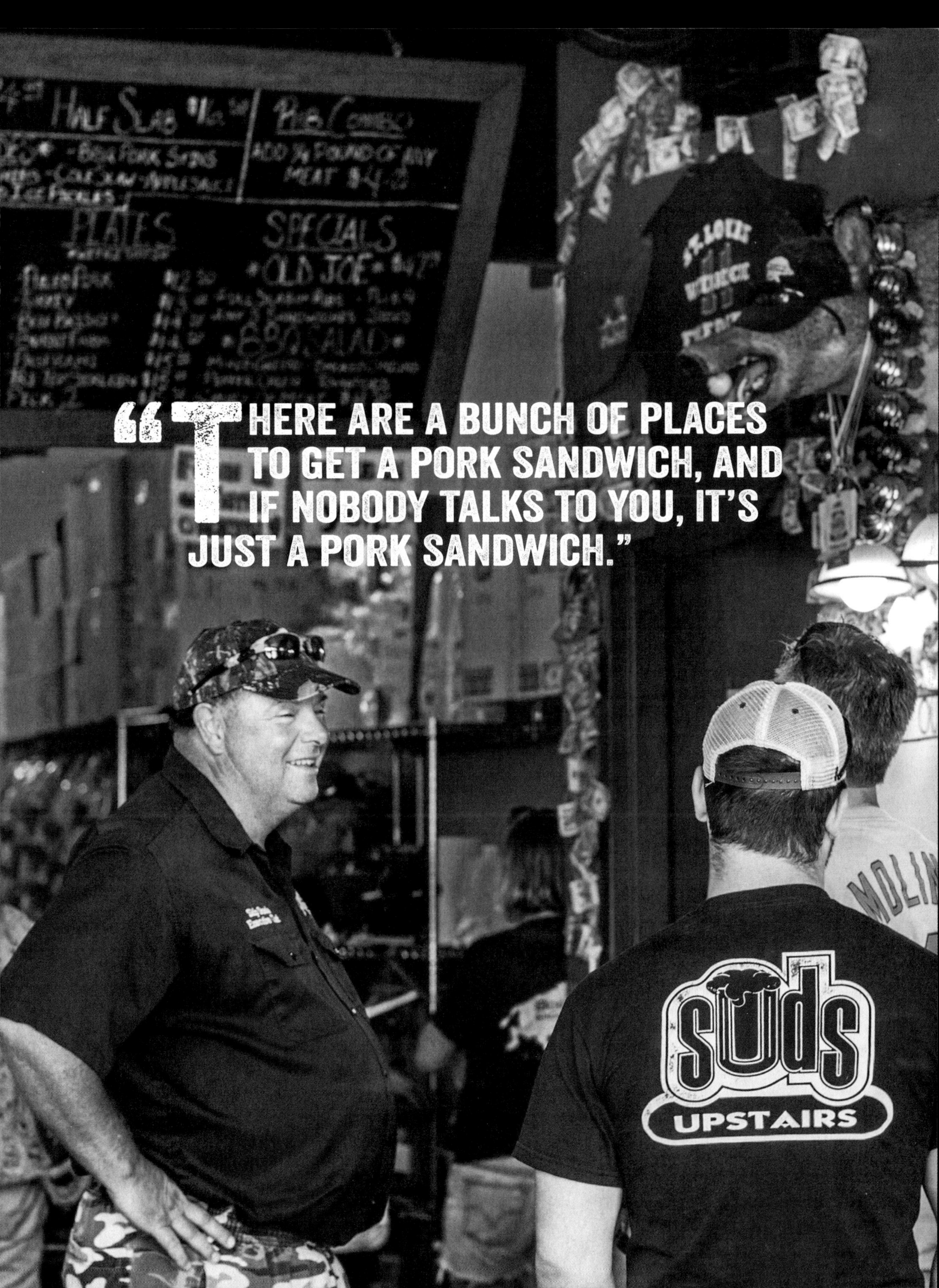

"THERE ARE A BUNCH OF PLACES TO GET A PORK SANDWICH, AND IF NOBODY TALKS TO YOU, IT'S JUST A PORK SANDWICH."

BURN CO. BARBECUE ♦ TULSA, OKLAHOMA

WALKING INTO BURN CO. BARBECUE IN TULSA'S 18TH AND BOSTON NEIGHBORHOOD IS AKIN TO GETTING BARBECUE BAPTISM BY FIRE. SURE, THERE ARE THE FAMILIAR ASPECTS—THINGS YOU'D EXPECT IN ANY BARBECUE JOINT, LIKE THE HICKORY AND CHARCOAL SMOKE THAT PERFUMES THE AIR OR THE LONG LINE OF FOLKS PATIENTLY, AND NOT SO PATIENTLY, WAITING OUTSIDE THAT TELL YOU THIS IS AN ESTABLISHMENT WORTHY OF YOUR TIME. BUT THEN THERE'S THE UNEXPECTED: THE OFFBEAT NOTES OF DISTORTED GUITAR—EITHER BOB MARLEY OR SUBLIME—MET WITH QUARTER NOTES OF KNIVES CHOPPING BRISKET, SAUSAGE, AND FATTY BY HAND.

In the background, you see nearly a dozen Hasty-Bake grills letting off a constant stream of smoke. And in the foreground, you'll find owner and pitmaster Adam Myers, along with his partner Nick Corcoran, standing over a butcher block and facing each other as if they are about to square off in an old-fashioned duel. It's frantic, fast-paced, loud, and—dare I say—exciting. These guys aren't slow dripping with molasses and sad country songs. They cook hot and fast. And the food tastes damn good too.

Just as I'm beginning to familiarize myself with my new surroundings, a group of five or so young GIs approach the counter. Taking his eyes off his moving knife and hands, Adam shouts, "Hey, you guys. Thanks for your service." He follows up with an offer. For a rate that sounds like the price of a cheap lunch in the 1930s, Adam promises the servicemen a plate of "a whole bunch of things." The platters he puts together are some of the largest assortments of food I've ever seen: ribs, pulled pork, Polish sausage, drumsticks, fatty, brisket, and smoked bologna, aka Oklahoma tenderloin. But the young bucks look happy to oblige, cleaning their platters quickly before rushing back to base.

Adam started Burn Co. Barbecue in 2012, in a smaller location, and the lines have yet to stop forming. "I fought working in the food business my entire life," Adam said, first pursuing a degree from Oklahoma State University, followed by a career in sales selling Hasty-Bake grills for 12 years. "A side effect of selling grills is that it led me to cooking," something he learned from Hasty-Bake founder Grant Hastings. After Adam initially struggled to meet his sales quota, Grant told him about the ol' show-and-tell sales technique—imploring that folks would buy a grill only when they could taste and see the results. The more Adam cooked, the more grills he sold—and the rest is history.

The more time I spend with Adam, the more I realize he's not about taking shortcuts. Take his smoking method. Adam falls back on his

love of lump charcoal, hickory chunks, and the Hasty-Bake grill. He and his team are constantly keeping close watch over the fire, ensuring the coals receive just the right amount of airflow to maintain temperature. "Every piece of meat here touches the fire," he says. Such a method is not easy, but you can taste the effort in every bite.

Nick tells me that being vertically challenged, aka short, is what helped him first land a job at Burn Co. Barbecue. No joke, the boys used to smoke their meats outside the restaurant in a trailer. Since the trailer door opening was shorter than normal, a person of any standard height was in serious danger of knocking himself out with the constant ebb and flow of managing the smokers. Nick is jokingly serious, but watching him chop meats and work the line tells me that Adam found a solid partner who commands a tall amount of respect. It's an expertise that Nick gleaned working for Richard Derner at The Hideaway restaurant while pursuing a degree at OSU in Stillwater, Oklahoma. Like Adam with Grant Hastings, a mentorship was built between Nick and Richard. Nick learned that life in the restaurant business could be all about family and fun.

You get a real sense from Adam and Nick that it's all about family at Burn Co. Barbecue. In addition to cooking the best food possible to provide for their own families, the boys often donate their time, food, and energy to serve local charities, public service men and women, and local businesses.

When pressed on what makes their BBQ unique, besides their fire-based methods, I'm reminded again of the regionalism of BBQ. Adam says, "the truth of the matter is that we all like what we grew up on." Adam tells me that Oklahoma BBQ is a bit of a "'tweener" style, taking nods from Texans' love for beef along with some of the sweeter sauces and beloved pork dishes of Kansas. Adam and Nick try to craft food that meets folks' needs, noting that there is really no right or wrong way to define good BBQ so long as it tastes delicious.

"OKLAHOMA BBQ IS A BIT OF A
''TWEENER' STYLE, TAKING
NODS FROM TEXANS' LOVE
FOR BEEF ALONG WITH SOME
OF THE SWEETER SAUCES AND
BELOVED PORK DISHES OF
KANSAS."

PORK BUTT

Pitmaster Adam Myers likens the pork butt to a dense, square mass. To shorten the cooking process and increase the surface area for more bark (flavor), he cuts the butt in equal halves. You'll notice he doesn't shy away from his Hasty-Bake days, preferring to utilize the tried and true rub and sauce of the namesake brand instead of creating his own. The Italian dressing is another trick out of the old man's book. The oil from the dressing helps to brown the meat while the vinegar plays a role in tenderizing. Overall, the dressing also helps to hold the rub. What is entirely all his, though, is technique. This butt is literally thrown into the fire, and the results, though unconventional, are fabulous. The meltingly tender pork has a sturdy, dark bark but is pliable and moist when pulled by hand.

SERVES 10 TO 12 • HANDS-ON: 20 MINUTES • TOTAL: 6 HOURS, 30 MINUTES

1 (6- to 8-pound) bone-in pork butt (Boston butt)
8 cups hickory wood chunks
¼ cup Italian dressing (such as Wish-Bone)
¼ cup dry seasoning rub (such as Hasty-Bake Original Flavor Rub n' Spice)
16 hamburger buns

1. Place the pork, fat cap up, on a flat surface. Cut the pork in half, parallel to fat cap. Using the shoulder blade as a guide, carefully cut underneath the bone to create 2 meat portions of equal size.

2. Light briquettes in a charcoal chimney starter. When the briquettes are covered with gray ash, pour them onto the bottom cooking grate of the grill and then push to one side of the grill. Scatter wood chunks over hot coals. Coat top cooking grate with oil; place on grill. Cover with grill lid, and heat grill to low (about 275°F).

3. Coat the outside of pork pieces with Italian dressing, and immediately rub on all sides with dry rub.

4. Immediately place the pork on prepared charcoal grill over direct heat. (Do not allow the meat to stand for any period of time once rubbed.) Grill, without grill lid, 1 hour, turning meat every 10 minutes. Transfer the pork to side of grate without coals, and grill, covered with grill lid, until a meat thermometer inserted in thickest portion registers 160°F, about 1 more hour, monitoring the meat and rotating often to prevent burning.

5. Tightly wrap each pork piece in foil, and return to side of grate without coals. Grill, covered with grill lid, until meat is falling apart and a meat thermometer inserted in thickest portion registers 210°F, about 3 hours.

6. Remove from grill, and let pork stand 30 minutes to 1 hour before serving. Remove bone and fat cap, and pull pork by hand. Serve with buns.

GRILLED POTATO SALAD

The potatoes pick up plenty of flavor and smoke from the well-seasoned grills, while the mix of onions and peppers provide a bright and welcomed contrast in this potato salad. The addition of bacon and reserved drippings takes this to a whole 'nother level—one that puts fork-to-mouth into autopilot mode.

SERVES 8 • HANDS-ON: 1 HOUR • TOTAL: 1 HOUR

3 pounds Yukon Gold potatoes, quartered
1½ tablespoons kosher salt
½ cup extra virgin olive oil
1 large red onion, cut into ¾-inch rings
2 large green bell peppers
1 pound bacon, cooked and crumbled, drippings reserved
⅓ cup spicy brown mustard
1 tablespoon apple cider vinegar
⅛ teaspoon fresh cracked black pepper

1. Coat cold cooking grate of grill with cooking spray, and place on grill. Preheat grill to low (about 275°F). Toss together the potatoes, salt, and ¼ cup of the oil until potatoes are well coated. Place the potatoes on oiled grates; grill, without grill lid, until tender, 25 to 30 minutes, turning occasionally. Remove from grill.
2. Place the onion rings and whole peppers on grates, and grill, without grill lid, until slightly blistered and tender, about 15 minutes.
3. Cut the grilled potatoes into 1 inch pieces, and place in a large bowl. Chop the onions and peppers, and add to potatoes. Add the bacon, reserved drippings, mustard, cider vinegar, black pepper, and remaining ¼ cup oil. Toss until combined, and serve immediately.

CANDIED BACON

This recipe will make you popular at your next dinner party. Myers prepares the bacon on the grill, but I find that baking it in the oven gives a more consistent result at home.

SERVES 6 • HANDS-ON: 10 MINUTES • TOTAL: 1 HOUR

1 pound hickory-smoked bacon
7 tablespoons firmly packed light brown sugar
½ teaspoon cayenne pepper

1. Preheat the oven to 300°F. Place wire racks in 2 rimmed baking sheets. Place the bacon slices in a single layer on racks.
2. Bake at 300°F until edges just begin to curl, about 20 minutes. (Bacon should still be pliable.)
3. Sprinkle the brown sugar evenly over bacon slices; sprinkle evenly with cayenne pepper. Return pans to oven, and bake at 300°F until sugar is caramelized and bacon is cooked through, 25 to 30 minutes.
4. Remove from oven, and cool completely, about 10 minutes. If desired, break into bite-size pieces before serving.

BURN
Tender Pulled Pork
Smoked Bologna
Chicken Drumsticks
Cheeseburger
Add a Meat - $3
Smoked Sausage

FATTY

Sometimes a name can tell you everything. Take this creation, for example: Sausage, upon sausage, upon sausage, all rolled up in bacon, and then smoked to fatty perfection. With the help of Craig Kus, the in-house butcher and sausage maker, this dish sets your taste buds into overdrive.

SERVES 6 TO 8 • HANDS-ON: 30 MINUTES • TOTAL: 3 HOURS, INCLUDING CHILLING TIME

Parchment paper
4 pounds ground pork sausage
2 (6-inch) kielbasa links
1 pound hot link sausage, minced
20 uncooked smoked bacon slices
(about 1¾ pounds)

1. Line a baking sheet with parchment paper. Shape the ground pork sausage into a 12-inch square, about 1 inch thick, on prepared baking sheet.
2. Place the kielbasa links, end to end, at 1 edge of ground pork sausage square. Gently roll the pork sausage over kielbasa just until kielbasa is completely covered.
3. Spread the minced sausage over remaining exposed pork sausage. Continue rolling from kielbasa end into a jelly-roll-style log. Chill 30 minutes to 3 hours.
4. Preheat gas grill to low (about 275°F) on one side, or push hot coals to one side of a charcoal grill.
5. Line another baking sheet with parchment paper. Arrange the bacon slices in a woven lattice design, with 10 vertical slices and 10 horizontal slices about ¼ inch apart, on prepared baking sheet.
6. Place the chilled sausage log at 1 edge of bacon lattice, and carefully roll up to wrap sausage log in bacon lattice. Fold bacon ends towards the bottom seam. If the bacon does not cover the entire log, fill in with extra pieces as needed.
7. Coat cold cooking grate of grill with cooking spray, and place on grill. Place the log, seam side down, on oiled grates over the unlit side of the grill. Grill, covered with grill lid, until a meat thermometer inserted in sausage log registers 165°F, about 2 hours. Remove from grill, and let stand 10 minutes. Cut into 2-inch slices, and serve.

r B Que
Heirloom Market
PITMAKER
Heirloom
Market BBQ
HEIRLOOM MARKET

HEIRLOOM MARKET BBQ • ATLANTA, GEORGIA

WHEN THE DEMAND TO EAT AT YOUR RESTAURANT SNARLS TRAFFIC TO A STANDSTILL, AND THE GEORGIA DEPARTMENT OF TRANSPORTATION THREATENS TO SHUT DOWN YOUR ESTABLISHMENT, THAT MY FRIENDS, IS WHEN YOU KNOW YOUR 'CUE STANDS TALL. THAT'S EXACTLY THE SCENARIO FACED BY HUSBAND AND WIFE CODY TAYLOR AND JIYEON LEE AT HEIRLOOM MARKET BBQ IN ATLANTA.

Established in 2010, Heirloom is housed in just 720 square feet, sitting adjacent to a convenience store where Cody and Jiyeon encourage patrons to purchase their own BYOB. Sweetwater 420 was my choice for the day.

With such a small footprint, great food, and overwhelming demand, the roads leading to Heirloom soon became so immobilized, the state of Georgia had to step in, forcing the establishment to become a "to-go" destination to ease turnover, and therefore traffic, though you are allowed to "stand as you can" and quickly enjoy your meal on the patio.

State government involvement is just one of the many "firsts" I encounter while visiting Heirloom Market BBQ. The second, and likely the most important, is that Cody and Jiyeon run one of the most respected BBQ restaurants in the country—and they do it together! Sheesh—making great BBQ is tough work, but doing it while married? That's impressive.

I suppose the last of the firsts, which explains everything, is the food. Heirloom is a whole new barbecue game of tastes and flavors. Some might say there's a rock star element to the food. But it would be more appropriate to label that element as less rock star and more Korean pop star. As it is written, Jiyeon happens to be one of South Korea's first and most famous pop stars. Cody tells me, "Jiyeon is the most famous Korean in Georgia." We all laugh, but he's dead serious. "Look her up."

But being a music sensation in her home country was not enough to satisfy her creative appetite. Upon moving to the United States in the late '90s, Jiyeon decided to express herself through food, first obtaining a culinary degree from Le Cordon Bleu in Atlanta, followed by stints at some of the city's most respected restaurants.

It was at one of those restaurants, Repast, where Jiyeon met Cody. Born in East Texas and raised in Knoxville, Cody snagged his first restaurant job around the age of 15. From there, he went on to pursue a culinary degree from The Art Institute of Atlanta, and like his wife, he worked his way up in some of Atlanta's finest kitchens.

Though separated by different countries, cultures, languages, and influences, the lesson is that you don't find love, it finds you. As I'm chomping down on the Spicy Korean Pork sandwich, I'm thankful for such fate, as their union benefits tens of thousands of hungry folks like me each year.

Let's get one thing straight. This is not Korean BBQ. At its core, Heirloom Market BBQ serves up a very traditional style of BBQ, influenced mainly by Cody's Southern upbringing and love of eating. This time, he's laughingly serious when he tells me he did plenty of "research" over the years, dining at over 500 BBQ establishments prior to opening Heirloom. Using a mix of Georgia oak and hickory, his smokers use only wood for heat and smoke—a definite labor of love.

Cody and Jiyeon use their training as professional chefs to maintain consistency and balance in what they serve. Instead of trying to turn BBQ into a form of haute cuisine, they simply use their hard-earned knowledge and experience to churn out food of the highest quality.

Though they never sought to create a fusion of American BBQ with a Korean influence, it just happened naturally. In fact, Jiyeon will tell you that she's long had a love affair for the traditional Southern meat and three, noting that much of the culinary, agricultural, and philosophical landscape of the American South mimics that of her home of Daegu, a rural south suburb of Seoul. Prepping collard greens one day, Cody asked Jiyeon to finish the dish. She braised the greens with a bit of rice wine vinegar and miso, and a new hybrid form

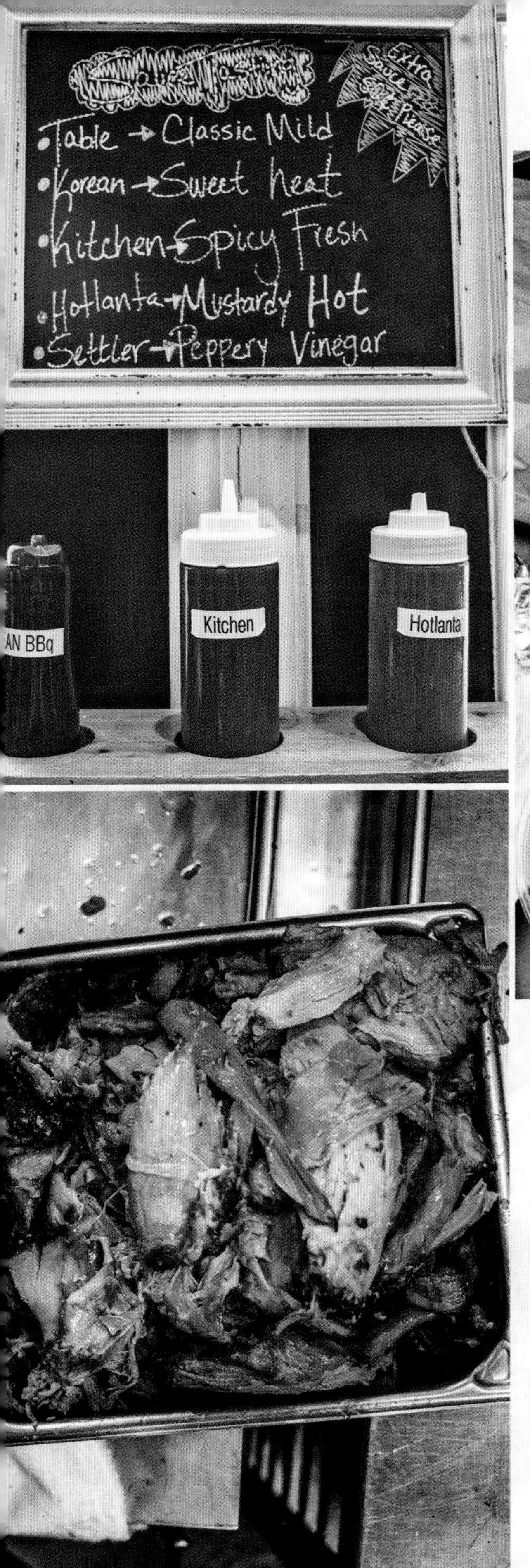

was born (just wait 'til you try these!). Such incidents continued to occur resulting in their unique fusion of 'cue. All that influence aside, the duo respect and pay homage to Georgia-style 'cue with a focus on pork and one heck of a Brunswick stew.

But for a city like Atlanta, once known as Terminus, where all railways of the South connected, Cody and Jiyeon are hopeful that their unique style can simply be viewed as Atlanta BBQ. When it comes to BBQ in Atlanta, all roads lead to Heirloom Market BBQ. And all that darned traffic is worth the wait!

8:01pm
SALT
Pepper
Pepper

SPICY KOREAN PORK

Cody uses a mix of Georgia oak and hickory to slowly smoke all of his meats in-house—no gas or anything else, just wood. In the early days, he experimented with many types of wood, finally settling on a mix of the two. Gochujang—used in the KB Sauce—is a red chili paste that serves as a Korean condiment of sorts. It's both spicy and savory, and it's something you can find fairly easily at most specialty markets. Cutting up the pork butt allows the maximum surface area to marinate overnight in the gochujang. From there, it's low and slow for a few hours until it reaches tender perfection. The finishing sauce adds the last and final complement to this unique-styled butt. Enjoy this pork on its own or on a potato bun with kimchi slaw, kimchi pickles, and KB Sauce. Trust me, the taste is truly worth the effort.

SERVES 14 • HANDS-ON: 45 MINUTES • TOTAL: 13 HOURS, INCLUDING CHILLING TIME

2 cups gochugaru (Korean red pepper flakes)
1 cup sweet chili sauce (such as Mae Ploy)
1 cup Sriracha chili sauce
¾ cup KB Sauce (page 88), plus more for serving
1 (8-pound) boneless pork butt (Boston butt), excess fat removed, cut into 1-inch-thick pieces
Wood chips
½ cup sliced scallions
3 tablespoons toasted sesame seeds

1. Stir together the gochugaru, sweet chili sauce, Sriracha, and KB Sauce in a large bowl. Add the pork; toss to coat. Cover and chill 8 hours or overnight. Remove the pork from marinade; discard marinade. Pat pork dry.
2. Prepare smoker according to manufacturer's instructions with an area cleared of coals to create an indirect heat area, bringing internal temperature to 225°F; maintain temperature for 15 to 20 minutes. Place wood chips on coals. Arrange the marinated pork in a single layer on grill rack over indirect heat. Cover with smoker lid. Smoke the pork, maintaining temperature inside smoker at 225°F, until pork is tender and a meat thermometer inserted into thickest portion registers at least 145°F, about 4 hours.
3. Remove the pork from smoker; let stand 10 minutes. Cut into small cubes. Drizzle with additional KB Sauce. Sprinkle with the scallions and sesame seeds.

KB SAUCE

Though the folks at Heirloom pride themselves on the quality of their smoked meat, they also offer up five sauces: Table (classic, mild), Kitchen (spicy, fresh), Hotlanta (mustard, hot), Settler (peppery vinegar), and the overwhelming favorite, KB Sauce, known as Korean BBQ sauce, which has a sweet heat. It's super unique and super addictive. So, fair warning.

MAKES 2¼ CUPS • HANDS-ON: 5 MINUTES • TOTAL: 25 MINUTES

1 cup (8 ounces) water
½ cup granulated sugar
⅓ cup firmly packed light brown sugar
3 tablespoons soy sauce
¾ cup lemon-lime soft drink (such as Sprite)
2 teaspoons gochujang (Korean red chile paste)
2 teaspoons sesame oil

Combine the water, sugars, and soy sauce in a medium saucepan; bring to a boil over high, stirring occasionally. Cool to room temperature, about 15 minutes. Stir in the soft drink, gochujang, and sesame oil. Store in an airtight container in refrigerator up to 1 week.

KIMCHI PICKLES

Making pickles at home means that you often have to wait days, weeks, or months until they can be enjoyed. I'm impatient, which is why I like these crunchy, slightly sweet, and tangy creations because they can be enjoyed immediately. That said, they get even better after a day or two.

MAKES 6 CUPS • HANDS-ON: 10 MINUTES • TOTAL: 2 HOURS, 10 MINUTES

2 pounds Kirby cucumbers
1½ tablespoons kosher salt
1 cup Kimchi Base Sauce (page 90)
½ cup thinly sliced onion
2 teaspoons granulated sugar

1. Cut the cucumbers into ¼-inch-thick slices using a mandoline. Combine the sliced cucumbers and salt in a bowl; let stand 2 hours. Drain and rinse with cold running water; pat dry.
2. Stir together the cucumbers, Kimchi Base Sauce, onion, and sugar. Serve immediately, or store in an airtight container in refrigerator up to 1 week.

"JIYEON IS THE MOST FAMOUS KOREAN IN GEORGIA. LOOK HER UP."

KIMCHI SLAW

A massive ice storm hit Atlanta months after Heirloom opened. With such limited indoor space, the storage refrigerators are situated outside, which caused a good bit of fresh goods to freeze. Jiyeon tells me that they were too broke at the time to buy a ton of new products, so she used a trick from her childhood of using frozen cabbage in kimchi, something they did during the harsh Korean winters. With plenty of frozen cabbage on hand, they came up with this hybrid recipe to serve as their own Heirloom-style coleslaw. And just like that, sometimes necessity and improvisation deliver a culinary masterpiece. You may, of course, use fresh cabbage in this recipe.

SERVES 12 • HANDS-ON: 15 MINUTES • TOTAL: 20 MINUTES, INCLUDING BASE SAUCE

1 (1-pound) head savoy cabbage, thinly sliced (about 8 cups)
2 cups thinly sliced scallions
2 cups thinly sliced carrots
½ cup Kimchi Base Sauce (recipe below)
1 tablespoon unseasoned rice vinegar

Combine the cabbage, scallions, carrots, base sauce, and rice vinegar in a large bowl. Serve fresh.

KIMCHI BASE SAUCE

6 garlic cloves
1¾ cups (14 ounces) water
1 cup coarse gochugaru (Korean red pepper flakes)
½ cup granulated sugar
¼ cup table salt
1 tablespoon freshly ground black pepper

1. Process the garlic and ½ cup of the water in a blender until smooth, stopping to scrape down sides as needed.
2. Whisk together the gochugaru, sugar, salt, black pepper, and remaining 1¼ cups water until sugar dissolves. Add garlic mixture. Refrigerate in an airtight container up to 2 months. Makes about 2½ cups

RICE WINE VINEGAR AND MISO BRAISED COLLARD GREENS

I'm always hankering for a good pot of collards, and this one certainly does not disappoint. In the early days, Cody prepped most of the side dishes. When he was too busy maintaining the smoker, Jiyeon stepped in and "doctored" up the greens. Cody sampled them, and being the smart married man that he is, told her exactly what she wanted to hear: They were great. Apparently customers thought so too—allowing these flavorful greens to remain a fixture on the menu.

SERVES 16 • HANDS-ON: 40 MINUTES • TOTAL: 1 HOUR, 40 MINUTES

8 ounces (1 cup) unsalted butter, cubed
½ cup vegetable oil
1½ pounds medium-size yellow onions, chopped (about 4¼ cups)
12 garlic cloves, minced
6 bunches (about 10 ounces each) collard greens, stems removed, leaves cut into ½-inch-thick slices (about 18 cups)
4 cups (32 ounces) water
1½ cups (12 ounces) doenjang (Korean soybean paste)
¼ cup gochugaru (Korean red pepper flakes)
¼ cup all-natural MSG-free Korean beef soup stock
¼ cup freshly ground black pepper
2 cups (16 ounces) rice wine vinegar
2 pounds smoked turkey breast, chopped (about 7½ cups)

1. Heat the butter and oil in a large stockpot over medium until butter is melted. Add the onions, and cook, stirring occasionally, until soft, about 7 minutes. Add the garlic; cook, stirring occasionally, until fragrant, about 3 minutes.
2. Add the collards in batches, about 6 cups per batch, and cook until wilted before adding next batch. Gently stir in the water, doenjang, gochugaru, beef stock, and black pepper until well incorporated. Stir in the rice wine vinegar.
3. Bring to a simmer, stirring occasionally. Cover and reduce heat to low. Cook until tender, about 1 hour. Remove from heat, and stir in the smoked turkey. Serve with a slotted spoon.

SQUEALER'S
HICKORY SMOKED BAR-B-QUE

SQUEALER'S HICKORY SMOKED BAR-B-QUE ♦ MERIDIAN, MISSISSIPPI

WHEN I WALK INTO SQUEALER'S HICKORY SMOKED BAR-B-QUE IN THE NORTH HILLS NEIGHBORHOOD OF MERIDIAN, MISSISSIPPI, I'M IMMEDIATELY GREETED BY PITMASTER AND OWNER TERESA CRANMORE, EXCLAIMING, "HI Y'ALL, WELCOME TO SQUEALER'S." HER SOUTHERN DRAWL IS AS AUTHENTIC AS ANY I'VE EVER HEARD, AND HER GENUINENESS IS AS DRIPPING SWEET AS SWEET TEA. I'VE BEEN IN HER RESTAURANT FOR LESS THAN 30 SECONDS, YET I FEEL AS WELCOME TO BE HERE AS ANY MEMBER OF HER IMMEDIATE FAMILY.

That's how things go at this joint. "I listen to my customers," Cranmore tells me, deadpanned and serious when I press her as to why Squealer's remains a local and statewide favorite for BBQ. It's not some canned interview response that she knows will sound good. She means it.

Her toughest customer, yet biggest supporter, has to be her husband, Terry. Let's get real: The female pitmaster is a rare breed. Most folks tend to associate BBQ as a man's domain, and Teresa will be the first to tell you that she owes a lot of her cooking credence and philosophy to Terry. Laughingly and still honestly serious, Teresa claims, "Terry used to tell me that sauce is something women put on meat that they've burned." I suppose 35 years of marriage allows one to make such statements and still remain married! That said, it's a philosophy that Teresa keeps close to heart while smoking and cooking her delicious meats, served sans any sauce, of course.

One of six children, Teresa was born and raised in Meridian, Mississippi, save for the fact that her father worked for the civil service, causing the family to do a stint or two abroad in Spain and the Philippines. Her mother was of Mexican descent, and she credits such influence on her Redneck Nachos and Smoked Quesadilla. Though she started her career working as an accountant, it was a love for people, family, and cooking that led her, now 17 years strong, into the restaurant business.

Teresa and Terry have built Squealer's from the ground up, fortified with a love for family, patrons, and faith. "My main ingredient is love," she says, "love for customers and a love to cook." Though the restaurant started out as a simple trailer placed next to a snowball stand, her passion for making the customer happy and taking criticism to heart is what she believes allowed her to build a thriving business and loyal customer base. "I'm not so vain as to think that I do everything perfectly," says Teresa. Such humility, honesty, and care for others are truly something you can taste in her food.

And then there are the pork rinds. The second greeting, besides the lovely Teresa, you receive

upon sitting down to peruse the menu is a basket of pork rinds. Teresa tells me that it's her own version of chips and salsa. They are delicious, life changing, and I cannot stop eating them. Seriously.

Then the onslaught of food comes—pulled pork, mac 'n' cheese, hand-cut French fries, ribs, and fried banana pudding. I'm grazing and eating all of it—gradually mixing a pork rind or two in for good measure. I'm stuffed on food and love.

But there's one more thing I have to do before leaving. It's an innate feeling that leads me to give Teresa a big ol' hug as though she were my own mama. It just feels natural.

She happily obliges, handing me a bag of pork rinds for the road.

"MY MAIN INGREDIENT IS LOVE," SHE SAYS, "LOVE FOR CUSTOMERS AND A LOVE TO COOK."

SQUEALER'S
BAR-B-QUE

SQUEALER'S PORK BUTT

Long, slow cooking and a methodical rub yield moist, tender pork. The hickory smoke really penetrates the meat, and the rub becomes a nice outer bark. Don't skimp on the rub. Teresa really gets it into every crevice. Her husband might joke about putting sauce on meat, this one is certainly worthy. Teresa doctors up a common store-bought sauce to create one that's a great complement to the meat. True to form, she has listened to her customers over the years to perfect the sauce based on feedback.

SERVES 10 • HANDS-ON: 20 MINUTES • TOTAL: 14 HOURS, 50 MINUTES, INCLUDING SAUCE

Hickory wood chunks
1 (8- to 10-pound) bone-in pork butt (Boston butt)
¼ cup Creole seasoning (such as Tony Chachere's)
Kaiser buns, toasted
Squealer's Original BBQ Sauce (recipe below)

1. Prepare smoker according to manufacturer's instructions, bringing internal temperature to 275°F. Maintain temperature 15 to 20 minutes.
2. Rinse the pork in cold running water, and pat dry. Rub the Creole seasoning on pork until liberally coated, making sure the fat cap is most liberally coated.
3. Smoke the pork, covered, over indirect heat, maintaining temperature inside smoker around 275°F, for about 14 hours or until a meat thermometer inserted in thickest portion registers 200°F.
4. Remove the pork from smoker; let stand 30 minutes. Remove and discard the bone and fat cap. Pull the pork by hand. Serve on the toasted buns with barbecue sauce.

SQUEALER'S ORIGINAL BBQ SAUCE

½ cup Cattleman's BBQ Smoky Base Barbecue Sauce
¼ cup ketchup (such as Hunt's)
¼ cup yellow mustard
¼ cup (2 ounces) white vinegar
¼ cup (2 ounces) Worcestershire sauce
1 tablespoon garlic powder
1 tablespoon freshly ground black pepper
½ cup (4 ounces) water
1 tablespoon cornstarch

1. Stir together the first 7 ingredients and ¼ cup of the water in a small saucepan. Bring to a boil over medium-high, stirring occasionally.
2. Stir together the cornstarch and remaining ¼ cup water in a small bowl. Add to the boiling sauce, and stir to combine. Return to a boil, and remove from heat. Cool before serving.
Makes 1½ cups

Squealer's Bar-B-Que
"Mississippi's BBQ Capital" – msn.com
Meridian's favorite family-owned
BBQ since 1998, Squealer's Hickory
Smoked Bar-B-Que believes
Bar-B-Que is a homemade style
of cooking that puts tender, juicy
meats front and center! Favorites
also include Beer Battered Onion
Rings, Fried Mac 'N Cheese,
finger-licking Wings and all the side
fixin's to go along. Wash it down with
sweet tea or a craft beer or spirit of
dessert try our homemade
Twinkies and Fruit Cobblers.
on the Front Porch each
at 6:30 p.m. – bring your
impeccable catering
Guest

REDNECK PORK NACHOS

A play on Teresa's Mexican heritage, these are to die for. The star of the show, of course, is the delicious pulled pork—generously layered over a serving of chips and then sprinkled with cheese and other tasty toppings. About halfway through, I actually started using some of the pork rinds to serve as my "chips." You could say I was eating high on the hog at that moment.

SERVES 4 • HANDS-ON: 15 MINUTES • TOTAL: 15 MINUTES

5 cups round tortilla chips
½ cup baked beans, warmed
10 ounces sharp Cheddar cheese, shredded (about 2½ cups)
6 ounces pulled pork
2 tablespoons sour cream
2 tablespoons sliced black olives
1 tablespoon Squealer's Original BBQ Sauce (page 100)
Toppings: dill pickle chips, sliced jalapeño chiles

1. Preheat the broiler with oven rack 6 inches from heat. Arrange half of the chips on a large ovenproof platter. Layer half of the beans, 1 cup of the cheese, remaining chips, remaining beans, and 1 cup of the cheese. Top with the pulled pork and remaining ½ cup cheese. Broil until the cheese is bubbly and slightly browned, about 5 minutes.
2. Top with the sour cream, black olives, and barbecue sauce. Serve with desired toppings. Serve immediately.

DEEP-FRIED PORK RINDS

I've never been to a place where pork rinds are served complimentary, and knowingly I ate half my weight's worth of these salty, spicy guys. Purchase dehydrated pork skins in pellet form online. After frying, these get dusted in a salt-and-cayenne pepper mixture.

SERVES 8 • HANDS-ON: 5 MINUTES • TOTAL: 5 MINUTES

Vegetable oil
½ tablespoon kosher salt
¼ tablespoon cayenne pepper
¾ cup medium-size pork rind pellets (such as Rudolph Foods Pork Rind Pellets)

1. Pour the oil into a Dutch oven to a depth of 3 inches. Heat over medium to 400°F. Stir together the salt and cayenne pepper.
2. Place the pork rind pellets in hot oil, in batches, and fry, pressing down occasionally to keep pellets submerged, until fully expanded and puffy, about 1 minute.
3. Transfer the pork rinds to a plate lined with paper towels to drain. Sprinkle with the salt mixture. Serve immediately.

FRIED BANANA PUDDING

Like my own mama, Teresa wasn't going to let me leave without having something "sweet." Her fried banana pudding is a customer favorite, and with one bite leading to another, and another, and another, I see why. The bananas hit a homemade batter and are fried until crisp and just warmed through. She tops the bananas with pudding, whipped cream, crushed vanilla wafers, and pecans. I'm honestly surprised they didn't have to roll me out of the restaurant.

SERVES 12 • HANDS-ON: 10 MINUTES • TOTAL: 30 MINUTES

5 cups all-purpose flour
4½ cups (36 ounces) whole milk
5 tablespoons (about 3 ounces) malt vinegar
4 teaspoons baking powder
1 teaspoon kosher salt
Vegetable oil
6 unpeeled just-ripe bananas
¼ cup powdered sugar
6 cups prepared banana pudding
Sweetened whipped cream
¼ cup crushed vanilla wafers
¼ cup chopped pecans

1. Stir together the flour, milk, vinegar, baking powder, and salt in a large bowl to form a thick batter. Pour the oil into a Dutch oven to a depth of 3 inches; heat over medium-high to 350°F.
2. Cut the unpeeled bananas in half crosswise, and cut halves in half lengthwise. Peel the banana segments. Dredge the bananas in batter until evenly covered.
3. Carefully drop the bananas in hot oil, in batches, allowing them to sink to the bottom. Fry for about 10 seconds. Using metal tongs, arrange bananas so that they are not touching each other or the surface of the Dutch oven. Fry until the bananas are golden brown, about 1 minute. Transfer the bananas to a plate lined with paper towels to drain. Repeat process with remaining bananas and batter.
4. Place 2 of the fried banana segments on each of 12 serving plates. Sprinkle evenly with the powdered sugar. Top with the banana pudding and 1 or 2 dollops of the whipped cream. Sprinkle with the crushed vanilla wafers and pecans. Serve immediately.

Helen's
BBQ

HELEN'S BBQ ● BROWNSVILLE, TENNESSEE

"I JUST DO."

THAT'S THE RESPONSE I RECEIVE FROM HELEN TURNER, OWNER AND PITMASTER OF HELEN'S BBQ IN BROWNSVILLE, TENNESSEE, WHEN I ASK HER HOW SHE COOKS. THERE'RE NO TRICKS, GIMMICKS, OR FOR THAT MATTER SHORTCUTS, BUT WHAT HELEN TURNER "JUST DOES" SURE TASTES MIGHTY FINE.

I should have expected such a curt response. When I press Helen on how she learned to "just do," she simply tells me to follow along. It's a hot and humid Tennessee afternoon, and I'm doing everything I can just to keep up with her—standing by her side as she flows from the back-of-the-house pit, to the kitchen, to the register, and of course, to chat with her loving customers. I'm starting to falter like a tired ole puppy dog—and Helen only seems to get more energized as the day presses on.

Helen must sense my fatigue, telling me, "Honey, you need to eat." She hands me a sandwich of smoked bologna, sliced as thick as a two-finger-high bourbon, topped with a crunchy slaw, and coated in a thin, spicy sauce. It is the best bologna sandwich I've ever had—and for those who know me—such a statement is rarely made. But damn, that thing is good. Sensing my revival, I'm met with an onslaught of food and kindness—spare ribs, chopped pork, and a Polish sausage all make their way into my mouth, and a whole lot of smiles and head nodding goodness ensues.

"I'm a firm believer that you can watch people do a lot of things—you can learn from that," Helen declares as we are maneuvering throughout her tight kitchen. Box fans swirl the smoke-filled air and cracklin' hisses and pops in an old cast-iron pot on the stove. Though I'm intently watching, I sense that I'll never really get the 'true' recipes from Helen.

Like my own mama, the fact is that neither she nor Helen writes anything down. They simply cook by feel and a whole lot of love. And when so many pitmasters and chefs rely on technology to produce perfectly consistent results, Helen laughs when she tells me, "The only thermometer I have in the restaurant is in the refrigerator."

Born and raised in Brownsville, Tennessee, a short stint outside of the famed BBQ hotspot of Memphis, Helen started working in this same establishment when it was formerly known as Curly & Lynn's. At the time, a man ran the pit, as you might expect. Over a decade, Helen learned by watching him, running the restaurant while juggling factory jobs. When it came time to take the helm over 20 years ago, she assumed the role of both owner and pitmaster and rechristened the restaurant Helen's. And trust me, though men might outnumber her in the pitmaster line of work, Helen certainly stands at the top of her field.

Her pit is as old-fashioned and crusty as any I've encountered throughout my travels, encased in cinder blocks, fastened and framed by steel, and fueled with a mix of hickory and oak. Helen tends to the fire throughout the day while also managing the restaurant. It's no joke, soot and smoke fill the air as we poke and prod at the coals. We're both sweating bullets as we discuss cooking methods and temperatures. Helen tells me her fire tends to run a bit hotter (300° to 325°F) than most other low-and-slow enthusiasts prefer.

When Helen steps back inside to finish taking orders, I spot a man out back fixing a hinge on a door. It's Helen's husband, Reginald. He tells me Helen isn't as tough and secretive as she pretends. He softens up, telling me that he views her as a jewel, soft-hearted and consistent. After receiving many hugs from Helen during my visit, I have to believe the man, even though I know I'll never pry the recipe for her tangy, sweet, and plenty-of-heat BBQ sauce from her!

Reginald is a huge part of Helen's success. He's not only a devoted husband, he wakes up at 4 a.m. to start the fire for Helen before running off to work his job as a group leader in the Haywood Company factory, a position he's held for nearly 40 years.

Prior to heading out, Helen needs one thing from me. I suppose I do owe her a favor, after harassing her all day about why and how her BBQ tastes so good. But I'm surprised when she asks me to sign a tattered wire-bound notebook. As I flip through the pages, I'm shocked at just how many folks, domestic and from abroad, have taken the time to come eat at Helen's. I see her filled with joy as she reads aloud the notes of praise from all of these friends and strangers.

I leave with one last hug, and I tell Helen that her food and positive effect on others is all worth the effort—so keep on doing what you "just do."

HELEN'S PORK BUTT

There's no rub or magic seasoning used to flavor this butt—just smoke. Helen cooks her butts a bit hotter than most, soaking up five or more hours of hickory and oak smoke. From there, she wraps the butts in foil and continues to cook them until they are meltingly tender. First pulled by hand, then expertly chopped with a knife, hers is one solid sandwich.

SERVES 10 TO 12 • HANDS-ON: 30 MINUTES
TOTAL: 11 HOURS, 30 MINUTES, INCLUDING COLESLAW AND SAUCE

8 cups hickory or oak wood chunks
1 (8- to 10-pound) bone-in pork butt (Boston butt)
16 hamburger buns
Coleslaw (recipe below)
2 cups Sort-of Helen's Sauce (page 112)

1. Prepare charcoal fire in smoker according to manufacturer's instructions. Place wood chunks on coals. Maintain internal temperature at 300° to 350°F for 15 to 20 minutes.
2. Rinse the pork, and pat dry. Smoke the pork, covered with smoker lid, 5 hours. Wrap the pork in aluminum foil, and return to smoker. Reduce heat to 275°F by closing vents halfway, and smoke pork for 5 hours. Remove from smoker, and let stand 1 hour.
3. Remove foil, and pull the meat by hand. Do not discard fat. Chop pulled meat with fat, and place on buns. Top each with 2 tablespoons slaw and 2 tablespoons sauce.

COLESLAW

By default, slaw is added as a topping for nearly every sandwich Helen serves. Its finely chopped texture and savory yet sweet flavor is a great complement to her smoky meats. It also stands up well on its own when served on the side.

SERVES 12 • HANDS-ON: 10 MINUTES • TOTAL: 10 MINUTES

1 (1-pound) head savoy cabbage, cored and quartered
2 carrots, peeled and halved crosswise
1 cup mayonnaise
¼ cup (2 ounces) red wine vinegar
1½ tablespoons kosher salt
1 tablespoon granulated sugar
½ tablespoon freshly ground black pepper

Process the cabbage and carrots in a food processor until finely chopped. Transfer to a bowl. Stir in the mayonnaise, vinegar, salt, sugar, and pepper, tossing to combine. Serve immediately, or cover and chill. Serve within 24 hours.

SORT-OF HELEN'S SAUCE

Neither you nor I will ever get the real recipe, but there are certain characteristics I tasted in Helen's sauce that allowed me to come up with my own version to suffice. Like most Memphis-based sauces, it's a melange of many BBQ influences: sweet and tangy, yes, but with a backbone of vinegar. Surprisingly thin, this sauce also packs plenty of punch with hot sauce.

MAKES ABOUT 2¼ CUPS • HANDS-ON: 30 MINUTES • TOTAL: 1 HOUR

1 ounce (2 tablespoons) unsalted butter
½ large Vidalia or other sweet onion, finely chopped (about 1 cup)
1 teaspoon freshly ground black pepper
2 teaspoons kosher salt
2 garlic cloves, minced
2 cups tomato sauce
¾ cup (6 ounces) apple cider vinegar
⅓ cup molasses
3 tablespoons yellow mustard
2 tablespoons Worcestershire sauce
2 tablespoons light brown sugar
1 tablespoon hot sauce (such as Crystal)

1. Melt the butter in a cast-iron skillet over medium-high. Add the onions, pepper, and 1 teaspoon of the salt, and cook, stirring often, until tender, about 10 minutes. Add the garlic, and cook, stirring constantly, 1 minute.
2. Stir in the tomato sauce, apple cider vinegar, molasses, mustard, Worcestershire sauce, brown sugar, and hot sauce; bring to a simmer over medium. Reduce heat to low, and cook, stirring occasionally, until slightly reduced and thickened, about 20 minutes.
3. Transfer to a blender, and add remaining 1 teaspoon salt. Remove center piece of blender lid (to allow steam to escape); secure lid on blender, and place a clean towel over opening in lid. Pulse until smooth. Cool completely, about 30 minutes. Refrigerate in an airtight container up to 1 month.

SMOKED BOLOGNA SANDWICH

You had me at bologna, but smoking it too? Now that's just not fair. Topped with slaw and sauce, this is the midnight snack I now crave. Helen lets the fire die down a bit to prevent burning this hunk of meat. Slice it extra thick and thank me later.

SERVES 12 • HANDS-ON: 10 MINUTES
TOTAL: 2 HOURS, 30 MINUTES, INLUDING COLESLAW AND SAUCE

Oak and hickory wood chips
1 (3- to 5-pound) bologna
12 hamburger buns
4 cups Coleslaw (page 111)
Sort-of Helen's Sauce (recipe opposite)

1. Prepare smoker according to manufacturer's instructions with an area cleared of coals to create an indirect heat area, bringing internal temperature to 300°F; maintain temperature for 15 to 20 minutes. Place oak and hickory chips on coals. Place the bologna on cooking grate over indirect heat. Cover with smoker lid. Smoke the bologna, maintaining temperature inside smoker at 300°F, until desired level of smoked flavor is reached, 2 to 2½ hours. (Be careful not to burn bologna.)

2. Cut the bologna into ½-inch-thick slices. Layer each bottom bun with 2 bologna slices, ⅓ cup coleslaw, and Sort-of Helen's Sauce. Cover with top buns, and serve immediately.

SMOKED POLISH SAUSAGE

If you call ahead, you can get an extra special treat of griddled peppers and onions added to this smoked sausage treat. Otherwise, Helen will serve it up traditionally with slaw and sauce. If you ask really, really nicely, Helen might also add some cracklin' on top. Best to call ahead or come early for both of those secrets.

SERVES 4 • HANDS-ON: 30 MINUTES • TOTAL: 1 HOUR, 30 MINUTES

4 (6-inch) kielbasa links (about 1 pound)
1 ounce (2 tablespoons) unsalted butter
1 Vidalia or other sweet onion, finely chopped (about 1½ cups)
1 green bell pepper, finely chopped (about ½ cup)
1 teaspoon kosher salt
1 teaspoon freshly ground black pepper
1 tablespoon water
4 hot dog buns
Sort-of Helen's Sauce (optional) (page 112)

1. Prepare smoker according to manufacturer's instructions, bringing internal temperature to 300°F; maintain temperature 15 to 20 minutes. Smoke the sausages, maintaining temperature inside smoker between 275° and 325°F, until a meat thermometer inserted in thickest portion registers 165°F, about 1 hour.
2. Meanwhile, melt the butter in a skillet over medium-high. Add the onion and bell pepper, and cook, stirring occasionally, 15 minutes. Sprinkle with the salt and pepper, and cook, stirring often, until onion and pepper are tender and nearly caramelized, about 25 minutes. Just before serving, add the water, and stir and scrape to loosen browned bits from bottom of skillet.
3. Remove the sausages from smoker, and slice sausages in half lengthwise. Place 2 sausage halves in each bun, and generously top with onions and peppers; drizzle with sauce, if desired.

PEAK BRO'S
BAR-B-QUE
Waverly, Ky.
PEAK BROS.
Buddy 1962
REFUSE

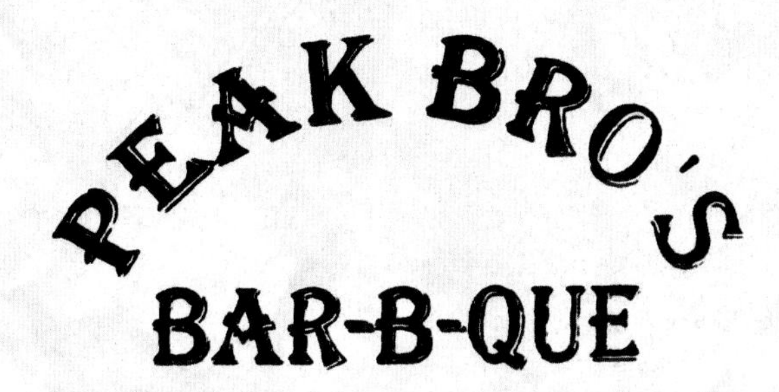

PEAK BROTHERS BAR-B-QUE • WAVERLY, KENTUCKY

PERSISTENCE. NOTHING IN THE WORLD CAN TAKE THE PLACE OF PERSISTENCE. ALTHOUGH FORMER PRESIDENT CALVIN COOLIDGE ONCE USED THOSE WORDS TO INSPIRE OUR YOUNG NATION, THE SAME SAID QUALITY OF PERSISTENCE COULD EASILY SIT SOLID AND SQUARE ON IRENE RICH'S SHOULDERS, THE OWNER OF PEAK BROTHERS BAR-B-QUE IN WAVERLY, KENTUCKY.

I learn about Irene's "one step in front of the other" mentality while downing a Waverly Waylay, a cocktail pink in hue and boasting six different spirits. Irene slowly draws on a Salem cigarette as she recounts to me the nearly 70 years of family history that have made Peak Brothers Bar-B-Que not only a staple of the community but also an icon of perseverance.

After returning from WWII, brothers Buddy and Barker Peak were in search of work. In those days, and still today, the town of Waverly, population of approximately 500, offered little more than farming or coal mining. The two brothers banded together what they could, first starting with a grocery business and eventually opening up Peak Brothers Bar-B-Que on July 4th, 1948.

Irene's father, Buddy, was known as a "character" in all realms. Irene recalls, "Honey, Daddy was one of a kind—he was a card—they threw away the pattern so nobody could remake him." The two brothers ran the business together for years until Barker stepped out and decided to run a gas station across town.

Barker's departure brought in partner Grover Greenwell, along with Buddy's kiddo clan of Irene, Debbie, Eddie, Tony, Bobby, and Billy Steve. Irene recounts that back then we lived in "a different era." The original 50-seat restaurant and bar served not only as a gathering place, but also as a local watering hole to grab a cold beer and a meal after working in the fields or the mines. In those days, men and men only were allowed in the bar.

As I sip on my second Waverly Waylay, locals begin to chime in with their own memories, including one-time Morganfield resident Jerry McKamey, recalling that Buddy Peak might in fact have pioneered the food truck business. It was a common sight to see Buddy hawking his hams, chipped mutton, and other goods at every community event, auction, or gathering.

Then comes the best memory from years past. Irene's eyes sparkle and her voice raises when she tells me about one of the greatest traditions at Peak's—the Coon Supper. "It was the place to be," she says, "an all-night affair held on Fat Tuesday of every year." As it was in those days, raccoons were hunted by the locals and gathered for the feast, baking and barbecuing the animals, along with sides of coon dressing, BBQ beans, and other trimmings. "All the food was free—you just had to pay for drinks," says Irene.

Such joyous memories turned to painful loss when Peak's was destroyed by fire in the summer of 1976. The original pits and a cash register were the only items that remained. With the support of his family, Buddy decided to rebuild the restaurant in 1977.

In the '80s, Buddy left the business, leaving it in the hands of Irene, Debbie, and Eddie. The siblings continued to carry on the tradition of Peak Brothers unique style of BBQ.

I suppose now is as good as any time to talk about the food. Peak Brothers Bar-B-Q has a long-standing tradition of using an open pit and hickory coals to smoke bone-in hams and mutton.

Those outside of Western Kentucky might find it strange to barbecue sheep, but the practice is quite common in the region. Irene believes it all got started with Catholic picnics. In those days, and still today, the Catholic community represents the vast majority of the folks in Waverly and the surrounding towns. Unlike pork or beef, mutton was always the most affordable meat to serve the masses. After being smoked, chipped, dipped, and cooked again, the meat is piled high and served with sliced Vidalia onions, dill pickles, and white bread. It's ridiculously delicious.

Irene will tell you that you come for the mutton, but you leave with a ham. Their smoked hams, rubbed with copious amounts of black pepper, are so famous that they were once shipped to First Lady Lady Bird Johnson. During the holiday season, it's not uncommon to place and locally deliver orders for over 2000 hams.

Unfortunately, the old saying that lightning strikes twice proved true in 2006 when Peak's was once again destroyed by fire. This time around, everything was destroyed.

With the support of her family and husband, who she lost in 2011, Irene said she "was crazy enough" to rebuild. "I've always loved this place—always have and always will." It's a love that Irene has passed on to her daughter Candace, who will serve as Peak's stewardess for the next generation.

Persistence and tradition indeed. After nearly 70 years of family business, surviving and rebuilding after two fires, living, loving, and losing loved ones, and serving as a trusted servant of the community, the tradition of persistence and "carrying on" has never tasted so good.

PEAK BROTHERS CHIPPED MUTTON

It might sound unorthodox to smoke a sheep shoulder (basically the "butt" of a sheep or lamb) but this practice has been a Western Kentucky staple for nearly a century. Typically, mutton (meat from sheep over 1 year old) is used, but younger lamb is more readily available and may be substituted. When finely chopped by hand, aka "chipped," it resembles the same texture as chopped pork or chicken. The shoulder is first smoked in an open pit over hickory until tender. After being chipped, the meat is "dipped" and placed back on the heat to impart even more flavor and tenderness. This two-step process yields a delicious treat to eat plain or smothered between two slices of white bread topped with crunchy raw onion and pickles.

SERVES 12 • HANDS-ON: 20 MINUTES • TOTAL: 9 HOURS, 40 MINUTES, INCLUDING DIP

Hickory wood charcoal
1 (7- to 8-pound) lamb shoulder
Peak Brothers Dip (recipe opposite)
White sandwich bread slices
Dill pickle chips
Thinly sliced Vidalia onion

1. Prepare smoker according to manufacturer's instructions, using hickory charcoal and bringing internal temperature to 325°F. Maintain temperature 15 to 20 minutes. (Or light charcoal in a charcoal chimney starter. When the charcoal is covered with gray ash, pour onto the bottom grate of the grill, then push to one side of the grill. Coat top grate with oil, and place on grill.)
2. Place the lamb on smoker or on oiled grate over indirect heat, and cover with lid. Smoke the lamb, maintaining temperature at 325°F, for about 5 hours or until a meat thermometer inserted in thickest portion registers 190°F. During last 2 hours of smoking, baste with Peak Brothers Dip every hour. Remove the lamb, and cover loosely with foil. Let stand 1 hour. Reduce smoker temperature to about 250°F.
3. Discard any bones or fat from the cooked lamb, and place the meat on a large cutting board. Using a cleaver or knife, chop the meat until finely diced.
4. Place the chipped meat in a shallow disposable aluminum foil pan, and stir in just enough of the dip to coat the meat, about 2 cups. (Do not overcoat.) Cover with foil, and return to smoker or grill grate over indirect heat, and smoke, maintaining temperature at 250°F, about 3 hours until very tender and sauce is absorbed, stirring every hour and basting with the dip if the meat looks dry.
5. Serve the chipped meat on white sandwich bread; top with pickles and onions. Serve with remaining dip.

PEAK BROTHERS DIP

"We don't call it sauce, honey," Irene tells me, "it's just called dip." It's a mix of vinegar and ketchup, with a bit of heat.

2 cups (16 ounces) white vinegar
¾ cup ketchup
1 teaspoon cayenne pepper
1 teaspoon kosher salt

Combine all the ingredients in a saucepan, and bring to a slow boil over medium. Allow the mixture to rumble and just reduce, about 10 minutes. Remove from heat, and serve.
Makes 2¾ cups

BBQ BEANS

Though most 'cue joints add smoked, pulled pork to their beans, Irene adds "chipped" smoked ham instead. The recipe for Peak Brothers smoked, bone-in hams is closely guarded, so you will have to sub your own smoked ham instead—something you can easily source at most supermarkets. The trick is to finely chop the ham and follow with a good soak in the dip, which imparts flavors into each and every bite.

SERVES ABOUT 12 • HANDS-ON: 10 MINUTES • TOTAL: 1 HOUR, 30 MINUTES, INCLUDING DIP

½ pound finely chopped smoked ham
½ cup Peak Brothers Dip (page 121)
4 (16.5-ounce) cans pork and beans
1 cup ketchup
½ cup firmly packed light brown sugar
½ cup finely chopped Vidalia onion
1 tablespoon yellow mustard

1. Preheat the oven to 375°F. Combine the ham and Peak Brothers Dip in a 2-quart baking dish; let stand 10 minutes. Stir in the pork and beans, ketchup, brown sugar, onion, and mustard.
2. Bake in preheated oven until bubbly and warmed through, about 1 hour. Remove from oven, and let stand 10 minutes before serving.

BEAN SOUP

I'm a sucker for soup, so when Irene puts this steaming bowl of bean soup in front of me on a hot Kentucky summer afternoon, I slurp it up until the bowl is polished clean, and then ask for a cold beer to cool back down. I'm a big believer that the simplest recipes are usually the best and such is the case with Irene's award-winning bean soup. I like adding a bit of dip (as you would a hot sauce) to add a punch of acidity and heat, prompting the necessity for yet another cold beer.

SERVES 6 • HANDS-ON: 5 MINUTES • TOTAL: 55 MINUTES

1 (16.5-ounce) can tomato juice
2 cups (16 ounces) water
1 large Vidalia onion, chopped (about 2¼ cups)
2 (16.5-ounce) cans white navy beans, drained
½ pound diced smoked ham (about 2 cups)
1 teaspoon kosher salt
½ teaspoon freshly ground black pepper

1. Stir together the tomato juice, water, and onion in a small stockpot, and bring to a boil over medium-high. Reduce heat to medium-low; cover and simmer until the onions are tender, about 15 minutes.
2. Add the beans and ham; cover and simmer until slightly thickened, about 30 minutes. Stir in the salt and pepper, and serve immediately.

IF USED BY
piggl

BIGG
BUTTS

BIG BUTTS BBQ ♦ LEACHVILLE, ARKANSAS

HANK WILLIAMS JR., ONCE CROONED THAT "SINGING ALL NIGHT LONG" WAS A FAMILY TRADITION. I'M PRETTY SURE HE MENTIONED A FEW OTHER TRADITIONS TOO. . . . FOR THE ROBERTSON FAMILY IN LEACHVILLE, ARKANSAS, ONE THING IS CERTAIN: BBQ IS NOT ONLY A FAMILY TRADITION—IT'S ALL BUSINESS.

Business and the town of Leachville, with a population of roughly 1,600 folks, made up mostly of those who work the land, have been good to the Robertson family. O.L. Robertson started a furniture business on Main Street in '55, and in the 80s, handed off the reins to his son Rodney. In true patriarchal fashion, Forrest is poised to continue the tradition if and when his father, Rodney, decides to ever stop working. Rodney's wife, Marti, calls him a workaholic in the most endearing of ways.

But furniture ain't the only gig in town for the Robertsons. A side effect of owning a furniture store meant that Rodney and Marti traveled far outside of Leachville to source for their business. Date nights out of town were always about eating out—a pleasure not much practiced in Leachville. So when they returned from their travels, the locals entrusted their palates to Rodney's cooking. And here's how they took that cue to develop their 'cue business.

Through trial and error, Rodney began to perfect his own method of Arkansas-style barbecue—with a focus on pork and charcoal smoking. Interestingly enough, he never used any wood for smoke or heat. For decades, the Robertsons' house served as a meeting place for folks from Leachville and surrounding communities to eat, meet, and greet. Such get-togethers served as a natural segue to opening up their own establishment nearly a decade ago.

Big Butts BBQ sits across from one of the country's largest cotton gins adjacent to a Dollar General store and amuck even more fields of cotton with a gravel drive and a parking lot that fills to the brim on Friday and Saturday evenings. Pulling up, it just looks like the kind of place that serves really good BBQ. Apparently, I'm not the only one who thinks so, as Marti tells me that folks from Tennessee, Arkansas, and nearby Missouri are all regular customers.

When you walk inside you start to get a sense of the Robertsons' dedication to not only their family, but also the community. Football jerseys and cheerleaders' uniforms from the local teams adorn the walls. And "regular" ain't a term to be taken lightly, as a group of retirees such as Ms. Motely, Pauly & Leon, Rita, and Eleanor are all likely to let you know if you've sat down at their table during a weekday.

There's probably no better way to sum up how you are treated at Big Butts other than with authentic Southern hospitality. I don't mean that in the "bless your heart" sentimentality that can saddle both truthfulness and irony. I take it straight from the big man himself when Rodney tells me that he tells his team to always go the extra mile. "Whatever they ask for, we accommodate," says Rodney. So when folks ask for "six pickles instead of four" or "the crust to be cut off their bread," Marti and her team of nearly 15 folks are happy to oblige.

But there's one more man on the payroll worth mentioning, Rodney and Marti's son Forrest, who serves as the caterer at-large and day-to-day pitmaster at Big Butts. Along with his new bride, ShaeLyn, Forrest is proving true that good parenting and apprenticeship are both worthwhile endeavors.

I get a sense that Forrest is wise beyond his young years as we are out back discussing his smoking technique learned from his father. He's worked hard to take the tools that his daddy provided, starting off their culinary adventure in a humble horse trailer, which also pulled a smoker, a rig that Marti eloquently describes as "Arkansas redneck." That said, Forrest has also stepped out on his own to create a style of 'cue that makes my taste buds sing "Glory, Glory." Seriously, just wait until you try the pork steak.

Besides the great food, support of the community, and the unique style of charcoal-fired 'cue, I must say that I'm left astonishingly satisfied by the overall joy and happiness of the

Robertson family. It's refreshing to see such a family business—firing on all cylinders—yet also devoted to the small town community that provides its support.

I'm also super, super full. And I do blame that on the Robertsons. Apparently, gorging oneself on such great food is another mantra of the family business.

As Rodney says, "If you leave here hungry, it's your own fault."

BIG BUTTS PORK BUTT

Big Butts BBQ relies on charcoal briquettes, not wood. Forrest tells me that the flavor is in the meat and the sauce. After the coals have turned gray, they are added to a rotisserie-style smoker heated surprisingly hot, 350° to 375°F. If you don't have a rotisserie, you can get the same effect by using indirect heat, with the butt set off as far from the heat as possible and turning from time to time. I've modified a version of Forrest's original sauce to complement his charcoal-smoked meats. The sauce at Big Butts is very thin—and vinegar forward. That said, it's got a good bit of heft and flavor that penetrates the meat in every bite. Hand chopped and sauced, this is one big butt—pun intended.

SERVES 10 TO 12 • HANDS-ON: 30 MINUTES • TOTAL: 6 HOURS, 45 MINUTES, INCLUDING SAUCE

1 (8- to 10-pound) bone-in pork butt (Boston butt)
Hamburger buns
Big Butts BBQ Sauce (recipe below)

1. Prepare smoker according to manufacturer's instructions, bringing internal temperature to 350°F to 375°F; maintain temperature 15 to 20 minutes. (Or light briquettes in a chimney starter. When the briquettes are covered with gray ash, pour onto the bottom grate of the grill, then push to one side of the grill. Coat top grate with oil, and place on grill. Place the pork on the oiled grate over the side without the coals.)
2. Rinse and pat the pork dry. Smoke the pork, covered, maintaining temperature inside smoker between 350°F to 375°F, for 3 to 4 hours or until a meat thermometer inserted in thickest portion registers 200°F. Wrap the pork in foil, and cook 3 to 4 more hours or until meltingly tender.
3. Remove the pork from smoker, unwrap, and pull the bone and fat from the pork. Use a large cleaver or chef's knife to chop the meat by hand.
4. Top bottom half of buns with 4 to 6 ounces of meat, and add a generous amount of sauce. Cover with bun tops. Serve immediately.

BIG BUTTS BBQ SAUCE

1 cup ketchup (such as Hunt's)
1 cup (8 ounces) white wine vinegar
1 tablespoon Worcestershire sauce
2 teaspoons kosher salt
2 teaspoons freshly ground black pepper
1 teaspoon smoked paprika
1 teaspoon garlic powder
1 teaspoon chili powder

Stir together all the ingredients in a saucepan, and bring to a simmer over medium. Reduce heat to low, and cook until just slightly reduced, about 10 minutes. Makes about 2 cups

1½"

BIG BUTTS PORK STEAK

Winner, winner, pork steak dinner. If you are weary of taking the time to prepare a whole butt, this should be your backup plan. Meaty, tender, and with so, so much flavor—this is definitely my go-to order at Big Butts. You can likely purchase these steaks at the store—most of the time they are named pork blade steaks. Otherwise, you could purchase a whole butt and ask the kind folks behind the meat counter to slice it into 1¼-inch steaks.

SERVES 6 • HANDS-ON: 1 HOUR • TOTAL: 3 HOURS

6 (1¼-inch-thick) pork butt steaks (about 3 pounds)
3 teaspoons kosher salt
3 teaspoons freshly ground black pepper
1½ cups Big Butts BBQ Sauce (page 128)

1. Light briquettes in a charcoal chimney starter. When charcoal is covered with gray ash, pour onto bottom grate of the grill, and then push to one side of the grill. Coat top grate with oil, and place on grill. Heat grill to 350°F.
2. Sprinkle the pork steaks evenly with the salt and pepper, and place over indirect heat. Grill, covered, 45 minutes. Place each steak on a large piece of aluminum foil, and top evenly with ½ cup of the sauce. Tightly wrap the steaks in foil, and grill, covered, about 1½ hours or until tender and a meat thermometer registers 205°F.
3. Remove the steaks from grill, and let stand in foil 30 minutes. Serve with remaining 1 cup sauce.

B-DADDY'S BBQ • HELOTES, TEXAS

MAKE NO BUTTS ABOUT IT . . . BEEF BRISKET IS THE SIGNATURE DISH OF TEXAS BBQ. IN FACT, JUST TRYING TO FIND ANY PORK IN THE LONE STAR STATE REQUIRED THE AID AND ASSISTANCE OF THE FBI. SERIOUSLY. FOR B.R. ANDERSON, OWNER AND PITMASTER OF B-DADDY'S BBQ IN HELOTES, TEXAS, JUST OUTSIDE OF SAN ANTONIO, COOKING UP A GOOD PORK BUTT MIGHT BE UNORTHODOX, BUT BREAKING SUCH TEXAS TRADITIONS HAD ITS GOOD INTENTIONS.

"Me? I never cooked a pork butt in my life," B.R. says, "but San Antonio is a military town—boasting at least five bases, which means I get folks stationed here from all over the country."

It was fate and good luck that led me to B-Daddy's. A childhood best friend, Justin Allbritton, was one of those transplant military men assigned to work in the San Antonio office for the FBI. So, when Justin claimed B-Daddy's to have the best BBQ in all of Texas, I told him to keep the beer cold and that I'd be there soon.

Now that I had my intel, I tried aimlessly to contact B.R. for weeks, but he skillfully avoided my calls, e-mails, and texts, telling me he was either "always working, or fishing and hunting on his ranch."

When we finally meet on a hot July afternoon, I realize B.R.'s deft skill and evasion tactics were honed at an early age. "I started racing BMX in '76, traveling all over the USA with my family in a motor home, eventually garnering a ranking as high as 5th in the World Championships in 1982."

Aha, it's all starting to make more sense, except for the name. After all, who goes by B.R.?

"I grew up Bernard Ray, and my younger brother, who also raced, and now runs USA BMX, was named Bernard Allen." One race day, the announcer got tired of distinguishing between the double monikered brothers, so he dubbed the nicknames B.R. and B.A.

After graduating on the "11-year-plan" with a marketing degree from the University of Texas at San Antonio, B.R. did a short stint selling industrial hoses before finally

transitioning to run a staffing business for roughly 20 years.

But life meanders, elevates, tabletops, declines, and rolls much like a good BMX course. In 2012, a divorce and midlife crisis led B.R. into realizing that he finally needed to do something for "me," he says. "BBQ saved my life."

I learned how to cook by watching my father." So for fun, B.R. and his college roommate Todd Pennington took a pit down to a BMX event in Houston. The day was so inspiring, B.R. went home, searched Craigslist, and bought a food truck in 2012.

After three months of sitting the truck on the side of Highway 281, B.R. felt more like a lone star than a rock star. "What have I done?" he asked, second-guessing his hasty decision.

With encouragement from friend Tom Robson, a local entrepreneur and restaurateur, B.R. put his marketing degree to work, advertising coupons on the back of grocery store receipts to gain more clientele.

The big break came when a regular customer, the president of the local Scorpions minor league soccer team, invited B.R. to take his truck to one of the games. While handing out samples, B.R. met another executive with the San Antonio Spurs who invited him to park the truck outside the arena at the first round of playoff games against the Lakers.

In a few short hours, B.R. and Tom sold more food than any other truck in the lot and were invited to every game thereafter.

It takes one bite of B.R.'s brisket for me to understand the hype. It's meltingly moist and tender, yet it holds together and never crumbles. The outer bark is pepper- and salt-crusted, and there's an overwhelming umami flavor that comes from the careful smoking process. And then there's the pork butt—smoked first, and drenched in Dr Pepper, then "pulled" with the help of an electric drill.

In 2016, B.R. moved into his permanent location in Helotes, still operating the original truck as his mobile satellite operation. One would be amiss to not recognize his right hand man, his son Kyle. Though his daughter Haley receives credit for the name B-Daddy, Kyle is a silent but steady force of the family operation. Like most young men, Kyle has ambitions of striking his own path one day, but he tells me earnestly that "spending time with Dad" is the greatest part of being in the restaurant business.

There you have it. Austin, Houston, Lockhart, and Dallas might reap most of the Texas BBQ attention, but down south in San Antonio, B.R. and the boys are cooking up venerable Texas classics, along with one good butt.

Don't believe me? Take it up with the FBI.

B-DADDY'S
BBQ
BR
B-DADDY'S
BARBEQUE

“BBQ
SAVED
MY LIFE.”

B-DADDY'S PORK BUTT

Prior to starting his food truck, B.R. Anderson had never cooked a pork butt in his life, but through trial and error, I'll tell ya, he does it some serious justice. His rub alone is a surefire hit on butts, ribs, pork chops, and turkey. He likes to smoke the butt until it forms a nice char on the outside. He transfers the butt to a pan, pours in a whole can of Dr Pepper, and continues to cook the meat until it's meltingly tender. These butts became so popular he had to find a quick and easy way to pull the meat. Some internet research led him to the RO-Man Pork Puller, a pronged device affixed to a drill. The process is quick and efficient.

SERVES 10 • HANDS-ON: 35 MINUTES • TOTAL: 15 HOURS, 15 MINUTES, INCLUDING RUB

1 (8-pound) bone-in pork butt (Boston butt)
¾ cup B-Daddy's Butt Rub (recipe below)
1 (12-ounce) can spicy, fruity cola soft drink (such as Dr Pepper)

1. Prepare smoker according to manufacturer's instructions, using live oak charcoal and bringing internal temperature to 225°F to 250°F. Maintain temperature 15 to 20 minutes. (Or light charcoal in a charcoal chimney starter. When charcoal is covered with gray ash, pour onto the bottom grate of the grill, and then push to one side of the grill. Coat top grate with oil, and place on grill.)
2. Rinse the pork, and pat dry. Using your hands, thoroughly work the dry rub all over the pork until evenly coated.
3. Place the pork, fat-cap side up, on smoker or on the oiled grate over indirect heat, and cover with lid. Smoke the pork, maintaining inside temperature between 225° to 250°F, for 6 to 8 hours or until a dark crust forms on the outside of the meat.
4. Remove the pork, and place in a deep aluminum pan; pour soft drink over pork. Cover with foil, and return to smoker or charcoal grill grate over indirect heat, and smoke about 8 hours or until a meat thermometer inserted in thickest portion registers 195°F. (The bone should pull easily from the shoulder when ready.)
5. Remove the pork from smoker, and let stand 30 minutes. Remove and discard the bone and fat cap. Using your hands, pull the pork into small pieces.

B-DADDY'S BUTT RUB

½ cup kosher salt
½ cup coarsely ground black pepper
½ cup chili powder
½ cup firmly packed dark brown sugar
½ cup granulated garlic

Stir together all the ingredients in a large bowl. Store in an airtight container up to 6 months. Makes about 3 cups

CLARA
Salt
Salt
Salt
Pepper
Pepper
Pepper

B-DADDY'S PULLED PORK TACOS

You can't visit Texas without having a taco, or three, as they are served at B-Daddy's. The deliciously tender and slightly sweet pulled pork is heaped in a warmed tortilla with creamy chipotle slaw.

SERVES 1 • HANDS-ON: 10 MINUTES • TOTAL: 10 MINUTES

1 ounce (2 tablespoons) unsalted butter
2 (6-inch) corn tortillas
6 ounces pulled pork, warmed
½ cup B-Daddy's Chipotle Slaw (recipe below)
2 tablespoons barbecue sauce (such as Head Country Barbecue Sauce)

1. Melt the butter in a large cast-iron skillet over medium-high until it foams. Add the tortillas, and cook until bottoms are lightly charred, about 30 seconds. Turn and top evenly with the pork; cook 30 seconds.
2. Remove the tortillas, and slightly fold. Top each with about ¼ cup of the slaw and 1 tablespoon of the barbecue sauce, and serve immediately.

B-DADDY'S CHIPOTLE SLAW

B.R. and his son Kyle have perfected this creamy, spicy slaw to serve not only as a topping for a sandwich or taco, but also as a formidable side. If you can't find chipotle salsa, simply blend up canned chipotle peppers in adobo sauce until smooth. If you have time, it's best to put this together a few hours before serving to really let the flavors meld.

SERVES 8 • HANDS-ON: 15 MINUTES • TOTAL: 15 MINUTES

½ head red cabbage, cored and finely shredded
½ head green cabbage, cored and finely shredded
½ red onion, thinly sliced
½ bunch fresh cilantro, finely chopped
½ bunch scallions, finely chopped
1 cup matchstick carrots
¾ cup mayonnaise
½ cup chipotle salsa
2 tablespoons honey
1½ tablespoons Sriracha chili sauce
1 tablespoon kosher salt
1 tablespoon freshly ground black pepper
½ tablespoon garlic powder
1 lime, juiced (about 2 tablespoons)

Combine all the ingredients in a large bowl. Using tongs or clean hands, thoroughly toss mixture until combined. Cover and chill until ready to serve.

B-DADDY'S BRISKET

B.R. shares my philosophy that great meals start with using great ingredients. For his signature brisket, he sources all-natural, hormone-free beef. From there, he lets a simple blend of salt and pepper serve as his seasoning, with expert technique to transform this tough cut into something so tender and flavorful it puts B-Daddy's in another class.

SERVES 20 • HANDS-ON: 30 MINUTES • TOTAL: 19 HOURS, 30 MINUTES

Oak charcoal
2 cups (6 ounces) coarsely ground black pepper
1 cup (3 ounces) kosher salt
1 (15-pound) beef brisket, deckle and kernel removed, and fat layer trimmed to about ¼ inch
Butcher or parchment paper

1. Prepare a large smoker according to manufacturer's instructions, using live oak charcoal and bringing internal temperature to about 225°F. Maintain temperature 15 to 20 minutes. (Or light charcoal in a charcoal chimney starter. When charcoal is covered with gray ash, pour them onto the bottom grate of the grill, and then push to one side of the grill. Coat top grate with oil; place on grill.)
2. Stir together the black pepper and salt. Rub the brisket with pepper mixture, ensuring every part of the brisket is thoroughly coated. Press the mixture into meat to adhere. Place the brisket, fat-cap side up, on smoker or on grill grate over indirect heat, and cover with lid. Smoke the brisket, maintaining inside temperature about 225°F, for 10 hours.
3. Remove the brisket, and wrap in butcher or parchment paper. Return the brisket to smoker or charcoal grill grate over indirect heat, and smoke, covered, 8 to 10 hours or until a meat thermometer inserted in thickest part of the large end registers 195°F.
4. Remove the brisket, and let stand wrapped in butcher paper 1 hour. Remove and discard paper. Cut across the grain into slices.

B-DADDY'S JALAPEÑO CREAMED CORN

Decadently simple, this slow-cooker side will be one of my go-to favorites for football season. In fact, the folks at B-Daddy's churn out SO much of this stuff, we had our work cut out for ourselves to literally cut the recipe to nearly 1⁄10 of its original size. Nevertheless, we did our work. Now do yours and go cook this up for your next family BBQ.

SERVES 8 • HANDS-ON: 10 MINUTES • TOTAL: 6 HOURS, 10 MINUTES

2 (8-ounce) packages cream cheese, cut into small pieces
1 (16-ounce) package processed cheese (such as Velveeta), cut into small pieces
4 ounces (½ cup) unsalted butter, softened
4 (16-ounce) packages frozen corn kernels, thawed
1½ cups (12 ounces) heavy cream
¾ cup (6 ounces) finely diced pickled jalapeño chiles
1 teaspoon kosher salt
1 teaspoon freshly ground black pepper
1 teaspoon garlic powder

Stir together all the ingredients in a 4-quart slow cooker. Cover and cook on LOW until the butter and cheeses are completely melted and well combined, 6 to 8 hours.

Guest Check
SERVER
TABLE
GUESTS
CHECK NUMBER
139201
ORIGINAL

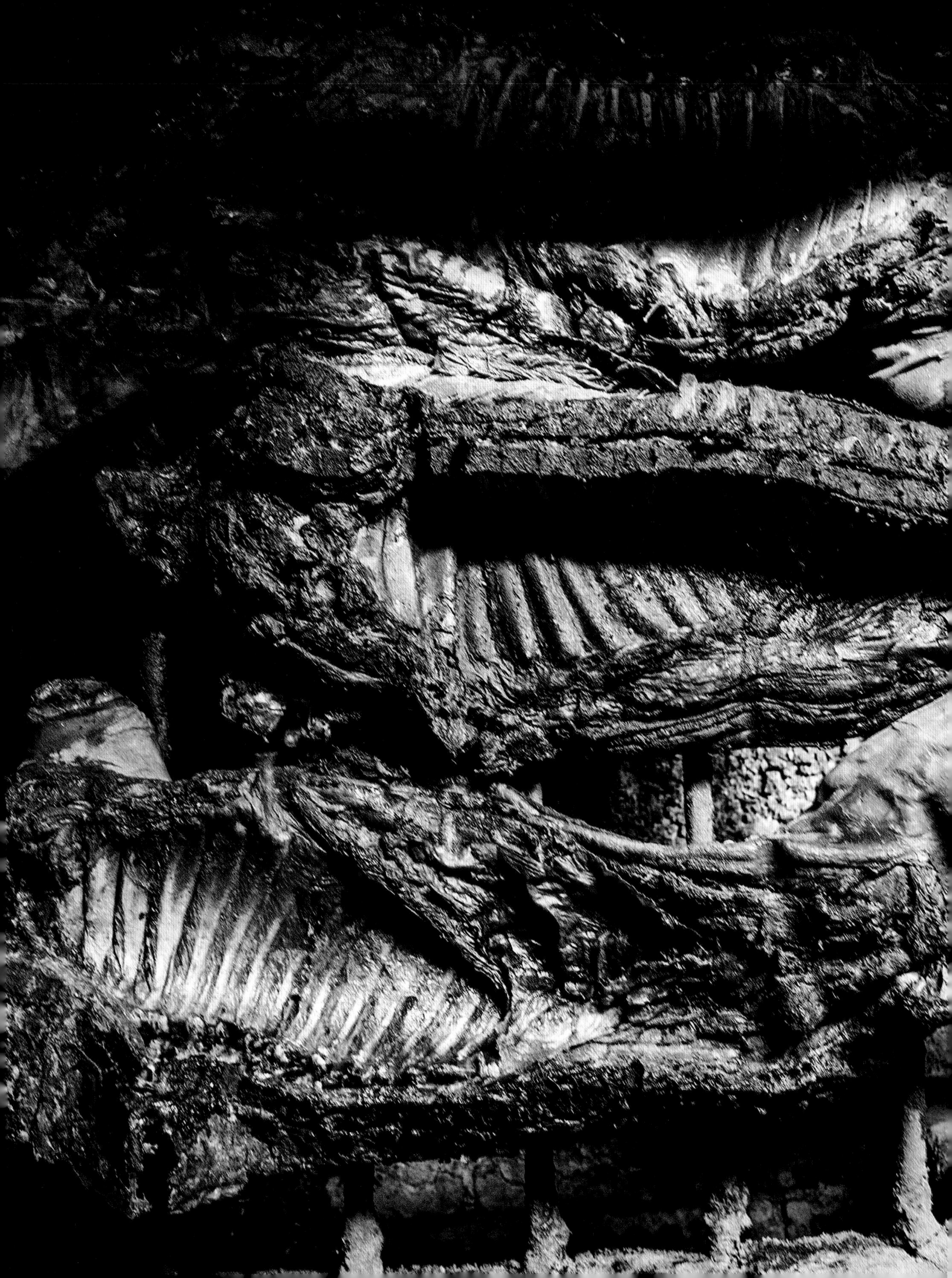

WILBER'S BARBECUE

WILBER'S BARBECUE ♦ GOLDSBORO, NORTH CAROLINA

"I WAS ALWAYS TOLD THAT YOU NEVER PUT KETCHUP ON PORK, OR VINEGAR ON BEEF." THAT MORSEL OF KNOW-HOW, SHARED BY WILBER SHIRLEY OF WILBER'S BARBECUE IN GOLDSBORO, NORTH CAROLINA, MIGHT SOUND UNASSUMING, BUT IT ELOQUENTLY DESCRIBES EASTERN CAROLINA BARBECUE TO A T. THEN, OF COURSE, ARE THE OPEN PIT, OAK COALS, AND WHOLE-HOG STYLE OF COOKING.

Wilber Shirley, or "Boss Hog" as he's known, needs no introduction. His barbecue has won more awards, critical praise, and long-term loyalty than nearly any other establishment where I've laid my taste buds.

Wilber grew up on a small tobacco farm in Kenly, North Carolina. He spent his youth farming and playing baseball, while also finding time to swoon his high school sweetheart Margie Barnes. His barbecue "journey" began in '49 when Wilber went to work for Lloyd Griffin at Griffin's Barbecue. It was there that Wilber learned the Eastern Carolina tried-and-true traditions that he still proudly practices today. Duty called in 1951, and Wilber was shipped off to Korea to fight the war. He served until 1954, and his uniform is still proudly displayed in his restaurant. After returning, Wilber reclaimed his post at Griffin's until 1962.

Wilber decided it was time to strike out on his own in 1962, partnering up with Carl Lyerly to purchase his own establishment from proprietor Fred Hill. After six months, Lyerly exited the business, yet Wilber remained.

On a good day, you'll enjoy Wilber's 'cue to the sound of chatter and gossip coming from the patrons seated at the countertop bar or the regulars who make up the "family table." On an even better day, the soaring sounds of F-16s will provide their own soundtrack as they perform "touch-and-go's" just a few hundred feet above the restaurant on final north pattern into Seymour Johnson Air Force Base.

When I arrive, Wilber, who is well into his mid-80s, has "business to take care of" prior to sitting down for a chat and a snack. I decide to let him make his rounds, while I mingle with the rest of the laid-back folk serving the continuous onslaught of

customers. I soon make my way over to Eddie Radford, who has been working for Wilber off and on for 52 years. "Don't believe anything he tells you," Eddie says with a smirk. "Naw, I'm just kidding . . . sort of," he reassures me.

Wilber might like to have a good time jesting with outsiders like me, but it's all business when he tells me that Eddie first came to work for him so he could earn money to pay for college, going on to become a school principal, then returning to Wilber's for "retirement." Eddie now serves as the "Master Dipper," a title that's displayed on the ordering board, in which he takes much delight.

Such longevity is a common theme at Wilber's. When I press another elder, Garry Price, on whether many soldiers stop in from the nearby base, he beams and tells me, "We always have room for one more."

Out back, I run into Leamon Parks, a wise and handsome man who has served with Wilber for 42 years, the last 30 of which he has spent chopping meat. To watch Leamon chop up whole hogs and shoulders is as beautiful as watching an artist render a famous work. I watch Leamon work two cleavers through the meat on a sturdy wooden board. Once it's reached the exact chopped consistency, he seasons the meat with fistfuls of salt, crushed red pepper, and warmed apple cider vinegar. Leamon tells me that his fistfuls are not an exact science, and the "Boss Hog" is known to get on him sometimes when the crushed red pepper reaches too much proportion.

"I believe in helping young people," Wilber tells me. In the beginning, he employed just 11 folks, with that number soaring to over 100 employees during many years. When Wilber survived a battle with prostate cancer, it was his family, employees, and customers that he treated so well that lifted him up with prayers and support to survive.

Sitting across from each other, I feel almost guilty for not writing down every word of advice from Wilber's lips, but I'm too darn busy stuffing my face with his perfectly spicy, vinegar-laden BBQ sopped up with a side of freshly fried hush puppies and drowned in sweet tea.

But I do find the time to stop eating to ask the most important question. When so many great men and women of Wilber's age are no longer with us, I find myself constantly trying to glean whatever experience and knowledge I can from this greatest generation. So when I query Wilber on what has been the key to his success, he confidently and succinctly tells me all I need to know.

"I have been blessed," he says.

“I WAS ALWAYS TOLD THAT YOU NEVER PUT KETCHUP ON PORK, OR VINEGAR ON BEEF.”

WILBER'S PORK BUTT SANDWICH

In North Carolina whole-hog is king, and at Wilber's you aren't getting just the butt, but bits of whole hog and butts chopped together for incomparable flavor. The classic Eastern Carolina vinegary tang of pulled pork is rounded out with creamy coleslaw in the sandwich.

SERVES 12 • HANDS-ON: 35 MINUTES • TOTAL: 14 HOURS, INCLUDING SAUCE AND SLAW

Oak charcoal
1 (8- to 10-pound) bone-in pork butt (Boston butt)
1 tablespoon kosher salt
1 tablespoon red pepper flakes
1 cup Wilber's Vinegar Sauce (recipe below)
12 hamburger buns
Wilber's Coleslaw (page 155)

1. Prepare smoker according to manufacturer's instructions, using charcoal. Bring internal temperature to 275°F, and maintain 15 to 20 minutes. (Or light charcoal in a charcoal chimney starter. When charcoal is covered with gray ash, pour onto the bottom grate of the grill, and then push to one side of the grill. Coat top grate with oil, and place on grill.)
2. Place the pork, fat-cap side up, on smoker or on grill grate over indirect heat, and cover with lid. Smoke the pork, maintaining inside temperature at 275°F, for 13 to 14 hours or until a meat thermometer inserted in thickest portion registers 195°F. Let stand 30 minutes to 1 hour.
3. Discard any bones or fat from the cooked pork, and place pork on a large cutting board. Using a cleaver or knife, chop the meat until finely diced, but not too overworked.
4. Stir the salt, red pepper flakes, and Wilber's Vinegar Sauce into diced meat; place on buns. Top with Wilber's Coleslaw, and serve.

WILBER'S VINEGAR SAUCE

2 cups (16 ounces) apple cider vinegar
1 teaspoon kosher salt
1 teaspoon red pepper flakes
½ teaspoon freshly ground black pepper

Stir together all the ingredients in a saucepan, and bring to a low simmer over medium-high. Remove from heat. Serve warm or at room temperature. Makes 2 cups

WILBER'S COLESLAW

Straightforward and simple, this slaw packs a punch, not to mention an addictive crunchy texture when added to a sandwich (optional) or served entirely on its own.

SERVES 6 • HANDS-ON: 10 MINUTES • TOTAL: 1 HOUR, 10 MINUTES

1 head green cabbage, cored and finely shredded
1 cup mayonnaise (such as Duke's)
1 tablespoon apple cider vinegar
1 tablespoon yellow mustard
1½ teaspoons kosher salt
1 teaspoon granulated sugar

Toss together all the ingredients in a large bowl until thoroughly combined. Cover and chill 1 hour.

WILBER'S POTATO SALAD

An evolving recipe that's mashed in texture and slightly sweeter than most. Wilber likes to boil the potatoes in the skin because they hold their shape and the skins slip off easily after cooking.

SERVES 6 • HANDS-ON: 1 HOUR, 5 MINUTES • TOTAL: 1 HOUR, 20 MINUTES

3 pounds russet potatoes (about 4 potatoes)
1 cup mayonnaise (such as Duke's)
1 tablespoon yellow mustard
1 tablespoon kosher salt
1 tablespoon apple cider vinegar

1. Bring the potatoes and water to cover to a boil in a large stockpot over high. Boil the potatoes until tender, 45 to 50 minutes. Drain the potatoes, and let stand until potatoes are cool to the touch, about 15 minutes.
2. Peel and dice the potatoes, and place in a large bowl. Add the mayonnaise, mustard, salt, and vinegar. Using a potato masher or whisk, mash the potatoes until they reach a smooth and incorporated consistency, with some potato chunks remaining. Serve immediately, or cover and chill until ready to serve.

BBQ CHICKEN

I'll be honest that the title of this dish, and what I ended up eating, is entirely a misconception. I figured I would receive smoked, or at least grilled chicken, slathered in sauce (I should note said preparation is one of the weekly specials). But instead, I ended up receiving something I wanted even more—slowly baked, tender, and moist chicken served with a light brown pan gravy. I'm not kidding when I say that this recipe is more guarded than any other at Wilber's, so I do my best to bring you this delicious dish, perfect for a Sunday supper.

SERVES 4 • HANDS-ON: 15 MINUTES • TOTAL: 1 HOUR, 10 MINUTES

2 (3½-pound) whole chickens, backbone removed, cut into quarters
2 tablespoons seasoned salt (such as Lawry's)
¼ cup all-purpose flour
1¼ cups (10 ounces) water
1½ tablespoons Wilber's Vinegar Sauce (page 153)

1. Preheat the oven to 350°F. Pat the chicken pieces dry; sprinkle with seasoned salt. Place the chickens, skin side up and in a single layer, in a large roasting pan. Bake, uncovered, in preheated oven until a meat thermometer inserted in thickest portion registers 160°F, 45 to 55 minutes. Transfer the chicken to a plate to cool, reserving drippings in roasting pan.
2. Place roasting pan on stove-top burners over medium-high. Whisk together the flour and ½ cup of the water in a small bowl. Add the flour mixture to pan, and whisk until combined. Stir Wilber's Vinegar Sauce and remaining ¾ cup water into the mixture; bring to a simmer. Reduce heat, and cook, stirring often, until reduced to about 1¼ cups, about 3 minutes. Serve the chicken ladled with pan sauce.

Diet Coke
Coca-Cola
Sprite

PER POUND

WRAP

Boiled Peanuts
WILBER

SHULER'S BARBECUE • LATTA, SOUTH CAROLINA

ON A DRIVE THROUGH LATTA, SOUTH CAROLINA, YOU'D BE HARD PRESSED NOT TO STOP AND GAZE WITH WONDER AT THE 130 FOOT TALL, 40 FOOT X 80 FOOT AMERICAN FLAG BEAMING UP FROM THE PARKING LOT OF SHULER'S BARBECUE. AFTER ALL, OUR NATION'S STARS AND STRIPES, ON SUCH A GRAND SCALE, ARE TRULY SPECTACULAR.

If you still need more convincing, just take a look at the line of folks wrapped outside the restaurant. As you begin to meander towards that line, I invite you to pause for a moment, and take in a deep breath or two of the heavy, humid South Carolina air. You should pick up trace scents of a sweat, an oak fire, and of course, the aroma of slow-cooked meats just ready to be devoured.

Latta sits just across the border from North Carolina, about an hour's drive inland from the coast, and roughly another 30 miles northeast of Florence, South Carolina—a city experiencing one of the most remarkable downtown revitalizations in all of our fair South.

Geographically, this area is named after the Pee Dee River, which takes its name from the Pee Dee Native American tribe. When I walk into Shuler's, I'm greeted by owner Lynn Hughes, who tells me that BBQ restaurants in this region are all commonly "buffet-style" establishments, typically open only on Friday and Saturday evenings.

Truth be told, I'm not much of a buffet guy. But the more time I spend at Shuler's, and of course, the more food I eat from the line, I find myself admiring the process. It's truly an art to maintain such quality, as they do, while also ensuring enough supply. Lynn's husband, Norton, the original pitmaster, sums it up eloquently with a drawl that's deep and sincere, "If they pay you for rib, and we run out, they ain't never gonna pay you for another rib."

Lynn and Norton both grew up in the Pee Dee. In fact Shuler's sits on the same land as Norton's family farm. Married nearly three and a half decades, the two rely on a lot of "give and take" in their relationship to run a successful enterprise—while also finding time to raise their son Shuler (named after Norton's father). I take a quick liking to Shuler, who just turned 12 and has more energy than a case of firecrackers.

Originally opened in May of 1996, Shuler's sat roughly 70 patrons. Since that time, they've expanded five times over, building a general store, banquet hall, and a bakery where I meet Lynn's mother, Lorraine Hamilton. "I started catering with Mama at 14, instead of getting in trouble," Lynn divulges while crediting Lorraine for many of the recipes that sit on the 25-plus-item buffet. That's all fine and dandy, but I've come for one of Grin-grin's (as Shuler calls her) most famous creations—her watermelon cupcake. It's seriously like a watermelon in your mouth—in cake form—with creamy white icing and chocolate chips. When I ask for the recipe, Lorraine replies, "bless your heart," which in Southern vernacular translates to over-my-dead-body. In other words, I might have purged a few of the family secrets, but I'm pretty sure that Lorraine's recipe for her delicious watermelon cupcakes will remain within the family—hence, go visit to give them a try.

After filling myself to the brim on a Friday evening, I return Saturday morning to sit down with Norton to chew the fat on all things BBQ. "We do not smoke," he tells me, "we barbecue, which means low and slow with the fat dripping on the coals for flavor." I used to say in college that nothing good happens after 2 a.m. and Norton shares my sentiment when he tells me that his fire should "never go above 240°F—that's my rule." Then there's his sauce. I've been waiting for it in all my travels—the beloved mustard. His, like many, is a hybrid, including mustard, while also inheriting much vinegar like his Northern kin. It's retail worthy.

In the smokehouse, I learn just what it takes to cook up so much food to serve the masses. Once designing his pits using actual size cardboard models to simulate the final build, Norton now regularly smokes 100 or more racks of spareribs a day. Of course, he's got a slew of pork shoulders, chicken, and other items "barbecuing" over the oak coals.

It might be large in quantity, but I can assure you, Norton's operation takes no shortcuts.

In the end, Lynn and Norton have created a restaurant that strives to provide great food with a focus on friends and family. "We work hard to serve people and make them happy," says Norton. For example, Lynn, a former elementary school teacher, earnestly tells me, "It's okay if the kids threw food at the wall. We'll be there to clean it up," she says with a smile.

I'll tell you though, the food doesn't need to hit the wall. Put it in your mouth, again and again, and be a real buffet pro and go back for a second round. Same goes for that dessert bar too!

Long live the buffet, and long live Shuler's Barbecue.

SHULER'S PORK BUTT

Low and slow, and never above 240°F, with the fat dripping on the coals for flavor—that's Norton's "secret" recipe for his deliciously tender pork butt.

SERVES 10 • HANDS-ON: 30 MINUTES
TOTAL: 13 HOURS, 30 MINUTES, INCLUDING RUB AND SAUCE

Oak charcoal
1 (8-pound) bone-in pork butt (Boston butt)
½ cup Shuler's Butt Rub (recipe below)

1. Rinse the pork, and pat dry. Work the rub mixture all over the pork butt.
2. Prepare smoker according to manufacturer's instructions, using charcoal. Bring internal temperature to 240°F. Maintain temperature 15 minutes. (Or light charcoal in a charcoal chimney starter. When charcoal is covered with gray ash, pour onto the bottom grate of the grill, and then push to one side of the grill. Coat top grate with oil, and place on grill.)
3. Smoke the pork, fat-cap side up, in smoker, covered, or on grill over indirect heat, maintaining temperature at 240°F, for 12 to 14 hours or until a meat thermometer registers 195°F.
4. Remove from heat, and cover with foil; let stand 1 hour. Discard bones and fat; pull pork by hand.

SHULER'S BUTT RUB

1¾ cups coarse kosher salt
1 cup medium-ground black pepper
½ tablespoon red pepper flakes
½ tablespoon cayenne pepper
½ tablespoon paprika
1 teaspoon garlic powder
1 teaspoon onion powder

Stir together all the ingredients in a bowl until incorporated. Use immediately, or store in an airtight container in a cool, dry place up to 6 months. Makes 3 cups

SHULER'S BBQ SAUCE

One taste of this mustard-vinegar hybrid sauce and you'll be thankful for the plentiful yield.

MAKES 6 PINTS • HANDS-ON: 15 MINUTES • TOTAL: 15 MINUTES

2 cups mustard (such as Sauer's)
12 cups (96 ounces) apple cider vinegar
1 teaspoon kosher salt
1 teaspoon freshly ground black pepper
1 teaspoon red pepper flakes

Simmer all the ingredients in a saucepan over medium-high, stirring occasionally. Cook for 5 to 7 minutes or until the mixture is slightly reduced. Remove from heat; serve warm or at room temperature.

SWEET POTATO SOUFFLÉ

I'm always a fan of counting your vegetables as dessert, which is how I'll chalk up this decadently sweet and delicious dish. Lynn tells me that this is one of the most consumed items on her buffet, and it's a simple family recipe she's proud to share.

SERVES 12 TO 16 • HANDS-ON: 1 HOUR, 10 MINUTES • TOTAL: 1 HOUR, 25 MINUTES

Sweet Potatoes
3½ pounds sweet potatoes, peeled (about 5 potatoes)
1½ cups granulated sugar
½ teaspoon kosher salt
¾ cup (6 ounces) fat-free milk
1½ teaspoons vanilla extract
5 large eggs, lightly beaten
Shortening

Topping
1 cup firmly packed light brown sugar
½ cup firmly packed dark brown sugar
1 cup self-rising flour
2 ounces (¼ cup) salted butter, melted

1. Make the potatoes: Bring the potatoes and water to cover to a boil over high. Cook until tender when pierced, 30 to 40 minutes, and drain. Place the drained sweet potatoes in a bowl, and beat at low speed with an electric mixer until mashed and slightly lumpy, about 30 seconds. Add the granulated sugar and salt, and beat on low speed until mixture is smooth, about 5 minutes.
2. Add the milk and vanilla, and beat on low speed until incorporated. Add the eggs, and beat until mixture is fluffy, about 1 minute.
3. Preheat the oven to 350°F. Grease (with shortening) a 13- x 9-inch pan. Pour the sweet potato mixture into prepared pan.
4. Make the topping: Stir together the light brown sugar, dark brown sugar, and flour until combined. Spread over the potato mixture. Drizzle with the melted butter.
5. Bake in preheated oven until the topping is lightly browned but center moves slightly, about 30 minutes. Serve immediately.

DEEP-FRIED CORN

Sometimes in life, you just don't know what you are missing. That's definitely the case with Shuler's deep-fried corn. Though you might first come to Shuler's to try the ribs, pulled pork, or mustard sauce, you'll keep coming back for the fried corn.

SERVES 6 • HANDS-ON: 10 MINUTES • TOTAL: 10 MINUTES

- Vegetable oil
- 6 ears fresh corn, husks and silks removed
- 1½ ounces (3 tablespoons) salted butter, melted
- 1 teaspoon kosher salt
- ½ teaspoon freshly ground black pepper

1. Pour the oil into a Dutch oven to a depth of 2½ inches. Heat the oil to 350°F over medium-high.
2. Carefully place 3 of the ears in hot oil, and fry, stirring occasionally, until slightly browned, 2 to 2½ minutes. Drain the corn on paper towels. Repeat with remaining corn.
3. Top the fried corn with melted butter (about 1½ teaspoons per ear), and sprinkle with salt and pepper. Serve immediately.

ALL the TRIMMINGS

SNACKS AND STARTERS

SMOKY BARBECUE POPCORN

Smoky, sticky, and sweet—these popped kernels are a true upgrade from anything you might find in a concession stand. Keep it simple with microwaved popcorn, or go old school and a bit more fancy by popping the corn on either a stove-top, or better yet, a smoker.

SERVES 8 TO 10 • HANDS-ON: 15 MINUTES • TOTAL: 15 MINUTES

3 ounces (6 tablespoons) salted butter
1 teaspoon Worcestershire sauce
1 tablespoon sugar
2 teaspoons smoked paprika
2 teaspoons chili powder
2 teaspoons garlic powder
2 teaspoons kosher salt
15 cups popped popcorn (from about ¾ cup kernels)

Melt the butter in a small saucepan over medium. Remove from heat, and stir in the Worcestershire sauce. Stir together the sugar and next 4 ingredients in a small bowl. Slowly drizzle the butter mixture over the popcorn, gently stirring as you drizzle. Sprinkle with the spice mixture, gently stirring to coat.

ROSEMARY SALT AND VINEGAR CHIPS

Say what you will about the store-bought version, this homemade brine really sets these chips over the top. I find that the brine used in this recipe is less harsh—and of course, more flavorful—than the packaged stuff. It's so much better that you can count on eating several handfuls.

SERVES 6 • HANDS-ON: 25 MINUTES • TOTAL: 25 MINUTES, PLUS 1 DAY CHILLING TIME

2 cups (16 ounces) malt or white vinegar
2 tablespoons sugar
2 tablespoons kosher salt
1 cup (8 ounces) water
2 large russet potatoes (about 2¼ pounds)
1 tablespoon finely chopped fresh rosemary
1 teaspoon freshly ground black pepper
Peanut oil

1. Combine the vinegar, sugar, 1 tablespoon of the salt, and 1 cup water in a medium-size glass bowl, stirring until the sugar dissolves. Cut the potatoes into thin slices, using a mandoline or sharp knife. (Cut them as thin as you can.)
2. Stir the potatoes into the vinegar mixture; chill 24 hours.
3. Stir together the rosemary, pepper, and remaining 1 tablespoon salt in a small jar. Drain the potatoes; gently pat dry with paper towels.
4. Pour the oil to a depth of 3 inches into a large Dutch oven; heat to 340°F. Fry the potatoes, in batches, stirring occasionally, 2 to 3 minutes or until golden brown. Drain on paper towels, and immediately sprinkle with the rosemary mixture. Serve warm, or cool completely (about 10 minutes).

SPICY QUESO DIP

Either dead sober, or after a few cold beers, cheese dip is one of my guiltiest pleasures. Naysayers, say what you will about a processed cheese blend, I'll let the results of this creamy and spicy dip speak for themselves in absolute deliciousness. Must. Have. Queso.

MAKES ABOUT 3 CUPS • HANDS-ON: 20 MINUTES • TOTAL: 20 MINUTES

1 small onion, diced
1 tablespoon vegetable oil
1 garlic clove, minced
1 (16-ounce) package pepper Jack pasteurized prepared cheese product, cubed
1 (10-ounce) can diced tomatoes and green chiles
2 tablespoons chopped fresh cilantro
Tortilla chips

1. Cook the onion in hot oil in a large nonstick skillet over medium-high 8 minutes or until tender. Add the garlic, and cook 1 minute. Remove from heat.
2. Combine the cheese, tomatoes and green chiles, and onion mixture in a large microwave-safe glass bowl. Microwave at HIGH 5 minutes, stirring every 2½ minutes. Stir in the cilantro. Serve with the tortilla chips.

Note: We tested with Velveeta Pepper Jack.

LOADED BAKED POTATO DIP

Amp up your traditional sour cream and potato vibe with actual, hearty ingredients. I like to bake my waffle fries extra crispy—that way they stand up to the creamy dip and let you scoop up all the garnishes without cracking under pressure. I highly encourage you to take a plunge into a dip so indulgent it's doubtful you can stop at just one bite! Anybody got a napkin?

MAKES ABOUT 4 CUPS • HANDS-ON: 25 MINUTES • TOTAL: 1 HOUR, 25 MINUTES

1 (2.1-ounce) package fully cooked bacon slices
2⅓ cups sour cream
8 ounces sharp Cheddar cheese, shredded (2 cups)
⅓ cup sliced fresh chives
2 teaspoons hot sauce
Garnishes: cooked, crumbled bacon; sliced fresh chives;
Waffle fries

Microwave the bacon according to package directions until crisp; drain on paper towels. Cool 10 minutes; crumble. Stir together the bacon and next 4 ingredients. Cover and chill 1 to 24 hours before serving. Serve with crispy, warm waffle fries. Store the leftovers in refrigerator up to 7 days.

"The Pig Skin" Deviled Eggs

Pimiento Cheese-Stuffed Pickled Okra

Texas Caviar
Deviled Eggs
Dixie Antipasto

DIXIE ANTIPASTO

Any veritable BBQ joint worth its salt will usually put out a spread of smoked sausage and cheese. I like to round out my assortment with whatever pickled items I have on hand—they not only are a crunchy treat, but their acidity helps to balance the fattiness of cheese and smoked sausage. Don't limit yourself to just the ingredients below—leftover pulled pork, brisket, or any variety of cheese always has a home on this platter.

SERVES 6 • HANDS-ON: 20 MINUTES • TOTAL: 20 MINUTES

1 pound hickory-smoked sausage (such as Conecuh)
1 (8-ounce) block sharp Cheddar cheese, cut into 1-inch cubes
1 (16-ounce) jar pickled pepperoncini, drained
1 sleeve saltine crackers
¼ cup coarse-grain mustard

1. Preheat the grill to 350° to 400°F (medium-high), or heat a grill pan over medium-high. Grill the sausage 5 minutes on each side or until slightly charred and grill marks appear. Cut the sausage diagonally into 1-inch pieces. Place on a large platter or serving plate.
2. Arrange the cheese, peppers, and crackers on platter with the sausage. Serve immediately with mustard.

PIMIENTO CHEESE-STUFFED PICKLED OKRA

Two of my favorite indulgences join in one harmonious marriage made in heaven.

SERVES 16 • HANDS-ON: 25 MINUTES • TOTAL: 30 MINUTES

1 pound Cheddar cheese, shredded (4 cups)
1 (7-ounce) jar diced pimientos
½ cup mayonnaise
1 tablespoon minced bread-and-butter pickles
1 tablespoon Dijon mustard
1 teaspoon kosher salt
1 garlic clove, minced
1 teaspoon cayenne pepper
2 teaspoons fresh lemon juice
2 dashes of hot sauce
Pickled okra pods
Garnish: smoked paprika

1. Stir together the shredded Cheddar cheese, pimiento, mayonnaise, pickles, Dijon mustard, kosher salt, garlic, cayenne pepper, lemon juice, and hot sauce in a medium bowl.
2. To serve, cut the desired amount of pickled okra pods in half lengthwise. Gently scoop out the seeds. Spoon the pimiento cheese into the okra halves.

TEXAS CAVIAR DEVILED EGGS

Greek yogurt, instead of mayo, serves as the base for this decadent mouthful. Since I've saved you a few calories with that substitution, feel free to spice things up a bit by adding a liberal amount of diced jalapeño.

MAKES 2 DOZEN • HANDS-ON: 30 MINUTES • TOTAL: 30 MINUTES

12 large eggs
⅓ cup fat-free Greek yogurt
2 ounces ⅓-less-fat cream cheese
3 tablespoons chopped roasted red bell pepper
1 scallion, minced
1 tablespoon chopped fresh parsley
1 tablespoon minced pickled jalapeño chile
1 tablespoon chopped fresh cilantro
1 teaspoon Italian dressing mix
1 teaspoon Dijon mustard
⅛ teaspoon table salt
Canned black-eyed peas
Fresh cilantro leaves

1. Place the eggs in a single layer in a stainless steel saucepan. (Do not use nonstick.) Add water to a depth of 3 inches. Bring to a rolling boil; cook 1 minute. Cover, remove from heat, and let stand 10 minutes. Drain.
2. Place the eggs under cold running water until just cool enough to handle. Tap the eggs on the counter until cracks form; peel. Slice the eggs in half lengthwise, and carefully remove the yolks. Mash together the yolks, yogurt, and next 9 ingredients until smooth, using a fork. Spoon the yolk mixture into the egg white halves. Top with the black-eyed peas and the fresh cilantro leaves. Serve immediately, or cover and chill 1 hour before serving.

"THE PIG SKIN" DEVILED EGGS

Eggs and bacon, or bacon and eggs. Either way you say it, there's no doubt that this is one delectable combo. I like to capture the game-day spirit by adding crispy pork crackling on top.

MAKES 2 DOZEN • HANDS-ON: 30 MINUTES • TOTAL: 1 HOUR, 30 MINUTES

1 dozen hard-cooked eggs, peeled
½ cup light mayonnaise
1 tablespoon finely chopped scallion
3 tablespoons sweet pickle relish
2 tablespoons sour cream
1 teaspoon spicy brown mustard
1 teaspoon Sriracha chili sauce
⅛ teaspoon table salt
Toppings: pickled okra slices, chopped pork crackling strips, chopped fresh parsley

Halve the eggs lengthwise, and carefully remove the yolks, keeping the egg whites intact. Mash together the yolks, mayonnaise, and next 6 ingredients until smooth, using a fork. Spoon the yolk mixture into the egg white halves. Top with the pickled okra slices, the chopped pork crackling strips, and parsley. Cover and chill 1 hour before serving.

BEER-BATTER FRIED PICKLES

Simple and delicious, this quick-fry method turns out a slew of pickles to serve hungry guests in no time. The spicy ranch dipping sauce ain't just for pickles—try it out on grilled veggies or even as a dipping sauce for smoked chicken wings.

SERVES 8 TO 10 • HANDS-ON: 25 MINUTES • TOTAL: 30 MINUTES, INCLUDING SAUCE

2 (16-ounce) jars dill pickle chips, drained
1 large egg
1 (12-ounce) can beer
1 tablespoon baking powder
1 teaspoon seasoned salt
1½ cups all-purpose flour
Vegetable oil
Spicy Ranch Dipping Sauce (recipe below)

1. Pat the pickles dry with paper towels.
2. Whisk together the egg and next 3 ingredients in a large bowl; add the flour, and whisk until smooth.
3. Pour the oil to a depth of 1½ inches into a large heavy skillet or Dutch oven; heat over medium-high to 375°F.
4. Dip the pickle slices into the batter, allowing excess batter to drip off. Fry the pickles, in batches, 3 to 4 minutes or until golden. Drain and pat dry on paper towels; serve immediately with the Spicy Ranch Dipping Sauce.

SPICY RANCH DIPPING SAUCE

¾ cup (6 ounces) buttermilk
½ cup mayonnaise
2 tablespoons minced scallions
1 garlic clove, minced
1 teaspoon hot sauce
½ teaspoon seasoned salt

Whisk together all the ingredients. Store in an airtight container in refrigerator up to 2 weeks.
Makes about 1 cup

COWBOY NACHOS

One thing is true about nachos: If you serve them, I will eat them. Adding in a hefty amount of smoked brisket and plenty of Monterey Jack cheese only increases said odds that I'll not only eat them, but likely ALL of them.

SERVES 6 TO 8 • HANDS-ON: 15 MINUTES • TOTAL: 1 HOUR, INCLUDING PICO DE GALLO

2 (16-ounce) cans seasoned pinto beans, drained
2 teaspoons hot sauce
1 teaspoon minced garlic
½ teaspoon freshly ground black pepper
½ cup (4 ounces) water
3½ cups shredded B-Daddy's Brisket (page 143)
1 tablespoon canola oil
½ cup (4 ounces) taco sauce
¼ cup meat drippings from brisket or beef broth
1 (9-ounce) package round tortilla chips
1 (8-ounce) block Monterey Jack cheese, shredded
Pico de Gallo (recipe below)
Toppings: guacamole, sour cream, pickled jalapeño chile slices, chopped fresh cilantro

1. Preheat the oven to 425°F. Cook the first 4 ingredients and ½ cup water in a medium saucepan, stirring occasionally, over medium-low 5 to 7 minutes or until thoroughly heated.
2. Heat the brisket in hot oil in a large skillet over medium, stirring often, 4 minutes or until thoroughly heated. Stir in the taco sauce and the pan drippings; cook 2 minutes.
3. Divide the chips, bean mixture, brisket mixture, cheese, and 1 cup of the Pico de Gallo among 3 pie plates.
4. Bake at 425°F for 5 minutes or until the cheese is melted. Serve immediately with the remaining Pico de Gallo and desired toppings.

PICO DE GALLO

6 plum tomatoes, chopped
½ cup finely chopped sweet onion
¼ cup chopped fresh cilantro
2 tablespoons fresh lime juice
1 jalapeño chile, seeded and minced
1 garlic clove, minced
½ teaspoon table salt

Stir together all ingredients in a medium bowl. Makes 3½ cups

CRISPY FRIED SWEET ONION RINGS

Either enjoyed on their own, or piled high on a pulled pork sandwich, fried onion rings are always a welcomed addition to any meal. Store any leftover dredging mixture (from Step 3) in an airtight container in the fridge up to two weeks—meaning you can fry up another batch when the craving returns! It's a good idea to ensure your oil is always at the proper temperature, especially between batches, to ensure the onions come out perfectly crispy.

SERVES 6 • HANDS-ON: 40 MINUTES • TOTAL: 2 HOURS, 40 MINUTES

2 large sweet onions, cut into ⅜-inch-thick slices
3 cups (24 ounces) whole buttermilk
Vegetable oil
2 cups all-purpose flour
1 cup plain yellow cornmeal
2 teaspoons table salt
½ teaspoon cayenne pepper

1. Separate the onion slices into rings, and place in a 9-inch square baking dish. Pour the buttermilk over onion rings. Cover and chill 2 to 24 hours.
2. Pour the oil to a depth of 2 inches into a Dutch oven; heat to 360°F.
3. Stir together the flour and next 3 ingredients in a shallow dish. Dredge the onion rings in flour mixture, and place on a baking sheet. Discard the buttermilk.
4. Fry the onion rings, in batches, 2 minutes or until golden, turning once. Drain on paper towels. Serve the onion rings immediately, or keep warm in a 200°F oven until ready to serve.

PETITE SWEET POTATO BISCUITS WITH PULLED PORK AND SLAW

These pulled pork slider biscuits are an acclaimed snack anytime of the year, but they really shine on a fall football weekend. The best part is that you can prep the biscuits weeks in advance—just freeze the dough until game day arrives. From there, thaw, bake, and top the biscuits with as much pork, slaw, and sauce as your heart desires. And, of course, pray for a win from the home team.

SERVES 12 • HANDS-ON: 20 MINUTES • TOTAL: 1 HOUR, 30 MINUTES, INCLUDING BISCUITS

1 cup finely chopped red cabbage
½ cup shredded carrots, chopped
1 teaspoon kosher salt
1 tablespoon mayonnaise
1 tablespoon red wine vinegar
⅓ cup barbecue sauce
¼ cup sliced scallions
Kosher salt and freshly ground black pepper
12 Sweet Potato Biscuits (recipe below)
1 ounce (2 tablespoons) unsalted butter, melted
½ pound pulled pork (without sauce), warmed
1 tablespoon chopped fresh chives

1. Toss together the first 3 ingredients in a small bowl. Let stand 30 minutes. Rinse and drain well. Whisk together the mayonnaise, vinegar, and 1 tablespoon of the barbecue sauce in a medium bowl. Stir in the cabbage mixture and the scallions. Add the salt and the pepper to taste.
2. Preheat the oven to 450°F. Split the biscuits, and brush with the butter. Place in a single layer on a baking sheet. Bake at 450°F for 5 minutes or until golden.
3. Top the biscuit halves evenly with the pork, remaining barbecue sauce, slaw, and chives.

SWEET POTATO BISCUITS

1½ cups mashed cooked sweet potato
1 cup (8 ounces) whole buttermilk
3 ounces (6 tablespoons) salted butter, melted
2 tablespoons sugar
⅛ teaspoon baking soda
3⅓ cups self-rising flour

1. Preheat the oven to 400°F. Lightly grease (with cooking spray) a baking sheet. Stir together the potato, buttermilk, and butter in a large bowl. Add the sugar, baking soda, and 3 cups of the flour, stirring just until dry ingredients are moistened.
2. Turn the dough out onto a lightly floured surface; knead 8 to 10 times, adding up to ⅓ cup more flour to prevent dough from sticking. Roll the dough to ¾ inch thick; cut with a 2-inch round cutter. Place the biscuits on prepared baking sheet.
3. Bake at 400°F for 15 to 20 minutes or until golden brown. Makes about 2 dozen

Wonder Wings with
Alabama White Sauce

Wonder Wings with Buttery Nashville Hot Sauce

Wonder Wings with Vietnamese Peanut Sauce

WONDER WINGS

The indirect and direct cooking method used in this recipe yields perfectly tender, moist chicken wings, with that sought-after crispy crunch from the skin. From there, the wonder sets in, sort of like a choose-your-own-adventure book, with your choice of four different dipping sauces to suit your palate. Truth be told, if you cook these guys as described below, they really don't need any sauce at all.

SERVES 6 TO 8 • HANDS-ON: 25 MINUTES • TOTAL: 1 HOUR, 10 MINUTES, INCLUDING SAUCES

3 pounds chicken wings
2 teaspoons vegetable oil
1 teaspoon kosher salt
½ teaspoon freshly ground black pepper
Alabama White Sauce, Buttery Nashville Hot Sauce, Vietnamese Peanut Sauce, or Buttermilk-Jalapeño Sauce (recipes follow)

1. Light 1 side of grill, heating to 350° to 400°F (medium-high); leave other side unlit. Dry each wing well with paper towels. Toss together the wings and oil in a large bowl. Sprinkle with the salt and pepper, and toss to coat.
2. Place the chicken over unlit side of grill, and grill, covered with grill lid, 15 minutes on each side. Transfer the chicken to lit side of grill, and grill, without grill lid, 10 to 12 minutes or until skin is crispy and lightly charred, turning every 2 to 3 minutes. Toss the wings immediately with desired sauce. Let stand, tossing occasionally, 5 minutes before serving.

ALABAMA WHITE SAUCE

⅓ cup mayonnaise
3 tablespoons chopped fresh chives
1 tablespoon prepared horseradish
4 teaspoons apple cider vinegar
2 teaspoons Creole mustard
1 teaspoon coarsely ground black pepper
¼ teaspoon sugar
1 garlic clove, finely grated

Whisk together the mayonnaise, chives, horseradish, vinegar, Creole mustard, pepper, sugar, and garlic in a small bowl. Makes about ⅔ cup

BUTTERY NASHVILLE HOT SAUCE

2 ounces (¼ cup) salted butter, melted
3 to 4 teaspoons cayenne pepper
2 teaspoons dark brown sugar
¾ teaspoon kosher salt
½ teaspoon smoked paprika
½ teaspoon garlic powder
1 tablespoon apple cider vinegar

Cook the butter, cayenne pepper, brown sugar, salt, paprika, and garlic powder in a small saucepan over medium, stirring constantly, 1 minute or until fragrant. Remove from heat, and stir in the vinegar. Makes about ⅓ cup

VIETNAMESE PEANUT SAUCE

3 large garlic cloves, finely chopped
1 tablespoon vegetable oil
⅓ cup (3 ounces) fish sauce
⅓ cup firmly packed light brown sugar
2 to 3 teaspoons Asian chili garlic sauce
3 tablespoons finely chopped toasted peanuts
¼ cup torn cilantro and mint leaves

Sauté the garlic in the oil in a small saucepan over medium 1 to 2 minutes or until golden. Stir in the fish sauce, brown sugar, and chili garlic sauce. Bring to a simmer over medium, and simmer, stirring occasionally, 4 to 5 minutes or until thickened and reduced to about ½ cup. Stir in the peanuts. Sprinkle the coated wings with the cilantro and mint leaves. Makes about ½ cup

BUTTERMILK-JALAPEÑO SAUCE

1 cup (8 ounces) refrigerated light buttermilk Ranch dressing
1 large jalapeño chile, stemmed
1 bunch fresh cilantro (about 1½ cups loosely packed)
2 garlic cloves, chopped
1 tablespoon fresh lime juice
Thinly sliced radishes (optional)

Process the Ranch dressing, jalapeño, cilantro, garlic, and lime juice in a blender or food processor 2 to 3 seconds or until smooth, stopping to scrape down sides as needed. Serve with wings and thinly sliced radishes, if desired. Makes about 1½ cups

SMOKED CHICKEN WINGS

Let me tell you, folks: you've never "brined" until you've brined in beer. Allowing the wings to soak overnight in this beer brine ensures that they will turn out plump and juicy on the grill. Because so much time, but not a lot of energy goes into this brine, choose a fruitwood like apple to provide just enough smoke to really let these guys shine. Save stronger flavored mesquite or hickory wood for another day. And since these wings spent the night swimming in booze, you should enjoy a cold one or two both while cooking and eating.

SERVES 5 • HANDS-ON: 20 MINUTES
TOTAL: 9 HOURS, 10 MINUTES, INCLUDING RUB AND 8 HOURS MARINATING TIME

2 (12-ounce) cans light beer
¼ cup kosher salt
¼ cup granulated sugar
2 tablespoons hot sauce (such as Tabasco)
4 bay leaves
2 pounds chicken wings
3 cups applewood chips (do not soak)
1 tablespoon olive oil
⅓ cup Wing Rub (recipe below)
Blue cheese or Ranch dressing (optional)

1. Combine the beer, salt, sugar, hot sauce, and bay leaves in a large bowl. Whisk the mixture until the salt and sugar dissolve; add the chicken wings, and toss to coat. Cover and chill at least 8 hours or overnight.
2. Tear or cut 1 (18-inch) square of heavy-duty aluminum foil; place the applewood chips in center. Fold foil to enclose chips. Pierce several holes in packet.
3. Heat 1 side of a gas grill to medium (300° to 350°F); leave other side unlit. Place the applewood foil packet on grate on lit side.
4. Remove the chicken from the beer mixture, and pat completely dry with paper towels. Toss the chicken with oil, and sprinkle with the Wing Rub, coating completely. Carefully move foil packet to grate on unlit side of grill. Place the chicken on grate on lit side, and grill, without grill lid, just until grill marks appear, 4 to 6 minutes. Transfer the chicken to unlit side of grill; carefully move foil packet back to lit side. Grill, covered with grill lid, until skin is golden brown and chicken is done, about 40 minutes, turning occasionally. Remove the chicken from grill, and let stand 10 minutes. Serve with blue cheese dressing or Ranch dressing, if desired.

WING RUB

1 tablespoon kosher salt
1 tablespoon paprika
1 tablespoon onion powder
1½ teaspoons ground cumin
1 teaspoon cayenne pepper
1 teaspoon garlic powder
1 teaspoon dried thyme
1 teaspoon dried oregano
1 teaspoon freshly ground black pepper

Stir together all the ingredients. Store in an airtight container up to 6 months. Makes about ½ cup

SMOKED PORK BELLY *with* SOY-LIME DIPPING SAUCE

Don't let the term pork belly weird you out. It's simply bacon in its presliced form. Now that we're clear, know that any good butcher can set you up with a hunk of pork belly. This recipe might require a bit of TLC, but like most things in life, the end results are definitely worth the journey.

SERVES 6 • HANDS-ON: 45 MINUTES
TOTAL: 14 HOURS, 45 MINUTES, INCLUDING SAUCE AND 12 HOURS CHILLING TIME

4 teaspoons kosher salt
2 teaspoons dark brown sugar
1½ teaspoons granulated sugar
1½ teaspoons paprika
¼ teaspoon garlic powder
¼ teaspoon freshly ground black pepper
⅛ teaspoon dry mustard
⅛ teaspoon ground cumin
1 (1¾-pound) pork belly
8 pounds hardwood charcoal
Hickory wood chunks
Parchment paper
Soy-Lime Dipping Sauce (recipe opposite)

1. Stir together the salt, sugars, paprika, garlic powder, pepper, dry mustard, and cumin. Sprinkle both sides of the pork belly with the seasoning mixture; rub to adhere. Cover and chill 30 minutes.
2. Prepare a charcoal fire with 4 pounds of the charcoal; let charcoal burn until covered with gray ash, 15 to 20 minutes. Divide hot coals into 2 equal piles, pushing each to opposite sides of grill. Carefully place 2 wood chunks on top of each pile. Place grate on grill. Place the pork belly, meaty side down and fat side up, directly on the center of grate without hot coals underneath. Cover with lid, leaving ventilation holes completely open.
3. Meanwhile, prepare an additional charcoal fire using 12 charcoal pieces of the remaining hardwood charcoal in a separate smaller grill or fire bucket. Let burn until covered with gray ash, 25 to 30 minutes. Carefully transfer hot coals from small grill to grill with the pork, placing 6 pieces each on top of each pile of hot coals. Add 2 more hickory chunks on each pile. Repeat process every 30 minutes.
4. Grill the pork, covered with grill lid, until a meat thermometer inserted into thickest portion registers at least 165°F (about 2 hours).
5. Remove the pork from grill, and place on a rimmed baking sheet. Cool completely, about 45 minutes. Cover the pork belly with a sheet of parchment paper. Place a large heavy skillet on top of parchment, and press down on the pork. Chill 12 hours (with skillet on top).
6. Cut the pork into ½-inch slices. Preheat a large cast-iron skillet over medium-high until hot; add the pork slices, and cook until crisp, 3 to 5 minutes on each side. Serve with the Soy-Lime Dipping Sauce.

SOY-LIME DIPPING SAUCE

¼ cup (2 ounces) soy sauce
2 tablespoons fresh lime juice
1 tablespoon fresh orange juice
½ tablespoon water
½ tablespoon mirin (sweet rice wine)
Red pepper flakes

Stir together all the ingredients in a small bowl. Cover and chill until ready to serve.
Makes ½ cup

BBQ PORK TAMALES

The tamale has served well the diet of many a Southerner, as it's the perfect "pocket meal" that packs plenty of flavor and sustenance. Though uniting the tamale with smoked pork butt is a bit unorthodox, one bite will make you a convert.

SERVES 12 • HANDS-ON: 45 MINUTES • TOTAL: 3 HOURS, 30 MINUTES

1 (3-ounce) package dried corn husks

Cornmeal Dough

1¼ cups shortening
6 cups fine yellow cornmeal
1¾ cups (14 ounces) warm chicken broth
2 teaspoons smoked paprika
¼ teaspoon kosher salt

Meat Filling

¾ pound pulled pork (without sauce), chopped (about 2¼ cups)
1 (10-ounce) can mild diced tomatoes and green chiles, drained
¾ cup bottled barbecue sauce
1 teaspoon garlic powder
1 teaspoon onion powder
1 teaspoon kosher salt
½ teaspoon cayenne pepper

Additional Ingredients

4 cups (32 ounces) water
3 cups bottled barbecue sauce
1 tablespoon chili powder
2 teaspoons ground cumin
Lime wedges (optional)
Fresh cilantro (optional)

1. Soak the corn husks in hot water until softened (about 1 hour). Drain the husks, and pat dry.

2. Make the Cornmeal Dough: Beat the shortening at medium speed with an electric mixer 2 to 3 minutes or until creamy. Stir together the cornmeal, chicken broth, paprika, and ¼ teaspoon salt in a medium bowl until well blended. Gradually add the cornmeal mixture to the shortening, beating at medium speed just until blended after each addition. Cover with plastic wrap; let stand 15 minutes.

3. Make the Meat Filling: Stir together the pork, diced tomatoes and green chiles, ¾ cup barbecue sauce, garlic powder, onion powder, 1 teaspoon salt, and cayenne pepper in a medium bowl.

4. Assemble the Tamales: Spread 3 tablespoons Cornmeal Dough into a 3½- x 3-inch rectangle in center of 1 corn husk. Spoon 1 tablespoon of the Meat Filling down center of the dough rectangle.

5. Fold 1 long side of husk over, completely enclosing the Meat Filling inside the dough rectangle. Fold short sides over folded and filled husk, and roll up, starting from the long folded side, to enclose the tamale. Repeat procedure with remaining Cornmeal Dough and Meat Filling.

6. Place a 1-cup ovenproof glass measuring cup upside down in center of a Dutch oven with lid. Stir together the 4 cups water, 3 cups barbecue sauce, chili powder, and cumin in a large bowl. Reserve 3 cups of the sauce mixture in a small saucepan. Pour remaining sauce mixture around measuring cup in Dutch oven.

7. Stand up the tamales around measuring cup. Bring the sauce mixture to a boil over medium-high. Cover, reduce heat to low, and simmer until the tamales are set, 2 hours to 2 hours and 30 minutes. Using tongs, remove the tamales to a serving plate.

8. While the tamales are cooling, cook the reserved sauce mixture in pan over medium-high until thickened and reduced to about 1 cup, 15 to 20 minutes. Serve the sauce with the tamales, and garnish with lime wedges and cilantro, if desired.

SIDEKICKS

SPICY OKRA FRIES

Take fried okra to the next level by serving it up in a French fried manner, alongside a tangy and fresh dipping sauce. Leaving the okra whole creates even more surface area for frying, ensuring these guys come out crispy and golden every time.

SERVES 4 TO 6 • HANDS-ON: 40 MINUTES • TOTAL: 45 MINUTES, INCLUDING SAUCE

¼ cup (2 ounces) fresh lime juice (about 2 limes)
2 tablespoons Worcestershire sauce
1 tablespoon dark molasses
Vegetable oil
2 pounds medium okra
2 shallots, minced
½ cup roasted peanuts, coarsely chopped
1 tablespoon garam masala
2 medium tomatoes, seeded and chopped
Cayenne pepper
¼ cup chopped fresh mint
¼ cup chopped fresh cilantro
Yogurt Sauce (recipe below)

1. Stir together the lime juice and next 2 ingredients until blended. Set aside.
2. Pour the oil to a depth of 2 inches into a Dutch oven; heat to 375°F. Fry the okra, in batches, 7 to 10 minutes or until crispy and deep golden brown; drain on paper towels.
3. Toss together the shallots, next 2 ingredients, okra, tomatoes, 3 tablespoons of the lime juice mixture, and cayenne pepper to taste in a large bowl. Sprinkle with the mint and the cilantro. Serve with the Yogurt Sauce and remaining lime juice mixture.

YOGURT SAUCE

1 cup plain Greek yogurt
1 teaspoon apple cider vinegar
2 tablespoons finely diced apple
2 tablespoons finely diced red onion
1 tablespoon chopped fresh chives
2 tablespoons fresh lime juice

Whisk together the yogurt and the vinegar until blended. Whisk in the apple, onion, chives, and lime juice. Makes about 1¼ cups

FRIED GREEN TOMATOES

A *Southern Living* classic recipe and a gold standard side dish of the South, the crispy cornmeal and flour crust is what really sets this recipe apart. I like to source firm, medium-size green tomatoes—they are hefty enough to fry, but not too tart.

SERVES 4 TO 6 • HANDS-ON: 30 MINUTES • TOTAL: 30 MINUTES

1 large egg, lightly beaten
½ cup (4 ounces) whole buttermilk
½ cup all-purpose flour
½ cup plain yellow cornmeal
1 teaspoon table salt
½ teaspoon freshly ground black pepper
3 medium-size green tomatoes, cut into ⅓-inch slices
Vegetable oil
Table salt

1. Combine the egg and the buttermilk in a medium bowl.
2. Combine ¼ cup of the all-purpose flour, cornmeal, 1 teaspoon salt, and the pepper in a separate shallow bowl or pan.
3. Dredge the tomato slices in remaining ¼ cup flour; dip in the egg mixture, and dredge in the cornmeal mixture.
4. Pour the oil to a depth of ¼ to ½ inch in a large cast-iron skillet; heat to 375°F. Drop the tomatoes, in batches, into the hot oil, and cook 2 minutes on each side or until golden. Drain on paper towels or a rack. Sprinkle the hot tomatoes with table salt to taste.

HERBED CUCUMBER AND TOMATO SALAD

Don't skimp on the herbs: fresh oregano, mint, parsley, and dill boost this simple salad into a delightful dish. And while I've got your attention, don't go cheap on the feta, either. I like to source a good goat's milk feta packed in brine. Trust me, you'll taste the difference.

SERVES 4 TO 6 • HANDS-ON: 15 MINUTES • TOTAL: 15 MINUTES

3 tablespoons extra-virgin olive oil
2 tablespoons red wine vinegar
1 teaspoon chopped fresh oregano
1½ pounds Kirby cucumbers, peeled, seeded, and sliced
1 cup grape tomatoes, halved
½ cup thinly sliced red onion
2 tablespoons fresh mint leaves
2 tablespoons fresh flat-leaf parsley leaves
2 tablespoons chopped fresh dill
Kosher salt and freshly ground black pepper
½ cup crumbled feta cheese

Whisk together the first 3 ingredients in a small bowl. Toss together the cucumbers, next 5 ingredients, and vinegar mixture in a large bowl. Season with the salt and the pepper. Sprinkle with the feta.

Fried Green Tomatoes

Herbed Cucumber and Tomato Salad

BACON + CORN HUSH PUPPIES

The only thing that could make a classic hush puppy even better is the addition of golden kernels of fresh corn and bits of crispy bacon. These textural, sweet-and-savory elements elevate this comfort food to extra special.

SERVES 15 • HANDS-ON: 25 MINUTES • TOTAL: 1 HOUR, 10 MINUTES, INCLUDING SAUCE

Vegetable oil
2 cups self-rising white cornmeal mix
¾ cup self-rising flour
¾ cup finely chopped sweet onion (from 1 small onion)
½ cup fresh corn kernels (from 1 ear)
½ cup diced cooked thick-cut bacon (about 8 slices)
⅔ cup (about 6 ounces) lager beer
⅓ cup (about 3 ounces) whole buttermilk
1 large egg, lightly beaten
Tartar Sauce (recipe below)

1. Pour the oil to a depth of 3 inches into a Dutch oven over medium-high; heat the oil to 375°F. Stir together the cornmeal mix, flour, onion, corn, and bacon in a large bowl. Add the beer, buttermilk, and egg; stir just until moistened. Let stand 10 minutes.
2. Using a 1-inch cookie scoop, drop a heaping scoop of the batter into the hot oil, and fry, in batches, until golden brown, 2 to 3 minutes, turning once. Drain on wire racks over paper towels. Keep warm in a 200°F oven. Serve with Tartar Sauce

TARTAR SAUCE

1 cup mayonnaise
1 tablespoon thinly sliced fresh chives
2 tablespoons chopped cornichons or other small dill pickles
1 tablespoon drained capers
1 large hard-cooked egg, peeled and chopped
1½ teaspoons fresh lemon juice
½ teaspoon cornichon juice from jar
¼ teaspoon dried tarragon, basil, or parsley
⅛ teaspoon cayenne pepper
Table salt and freshly ground black pepper

Stir together the mayonnaise, chives, chopped cornichons, capers, egg, lemon juice, cornichon juice, dried tarragon, basil, or parsley, and cayenne pepper in a small bowl. Add the salt and pepper to taste. Cover and chill 30 minutes before serving. Refrigerate up to 3 days.
Makes 1½ cups

Lowcountry Slaw

Jicama Slaw

Creamy Dill Slaw
Confetti Slaw

LOWCOUNTRY SLAW

Sometimes a shortcut in the kitchen can be a real time-saver without sacrificing the quality of the finished dish. Packaged, preshredded slaw mix is a perfect example. It saves loads of prep time. I'll owe you a beer if you can't have this dish on the table in less than fifteen minutes flat.

SERVES 4 • HANDS-ON: 10 MINUTES • TOTAL: 10 MINUTES

¼ cup (2 ounces) apple cider vinegar
¼ cup canola oil
2 tablespoons mayonnaise
2 tablespoons pickled okra juice
1 tablespoon honey
½ teaspoon table salt
¼ teaspoon freshly ground black pepper
¼ teaspoon celery seeds
1 (16-ounce) package shredded coleslaw mix
1 cup sliced pickled okra
Garnish: toasted pecan halves

Whisk together the vinegar, canola oil, mayonnaise, okra juice, honey, salt, pepper, and celery seeds in a large bowl. Stir in the coleslaw mix and the pickled okra. Serve immediately, or chill up to 24 hours. Garnish, if desired.

CONFETTI SLAW

Pops of nearly every color in the rainbow make their way into this slaw. Not only is this dish beautiful on the table, it also boasts a vinaigrette that keeps the components light and refreshing. Look to this as an ideal side dish to serve with any smoked or grilled meat.

SERVES 10 TO 12 • HANDS-ON: 15 MINUTES
TOTAL: 15 MINUTES, INCLUDING DRESSING, PLUS 2 HOURS CHILLING TIME

1 small cabbage, chopped
3 medium carrots, diced
2 celery ribs, diced
1 large green bell pepper, diced
1 large red bell pepper, diced
1 small cucumber, peeled, seeded, and diced
1 (6-ounce) bag radishes, sliced
1 large onion, diced
Slaw Dressing (recipe opposite)

Combine the first 8 ingredients in a large bowl. Add the Slaw Dressing, and toss to coat. Cover and chill at least 2 hours. Drain before serving.

SLAW DRESSING

1 cup (8 ounces) white vinegar
⅓ cup vegetable oil
¾ cup sugar
1 teaspoon table salt
¼ teaspoon freshly ground black pepper

Combine all the ingredients in a jar; cover tightly, and shake vigorously before pouring. Makes 1¾ cups

JICAMA SLAW

Often referred to as the "Mexican turnip," jicama root is starchy and slightly sour, similar to a green apple in taste and texture. I like to serve this slaw as a side, knowing full well that I also will eagerly use it as a topping on either a pulled pork sandwich or brisket taco.

SERVES 10 • HANDS-ON: 10 MINUTES • TOTAL: 10 MINUTES

2 cups shredded red cabbage (about ½ medium-size red cabbage)
2 cups thinly sliced jicama (about ½ medium jicama)
¼ cup thinly sliced red onion
¼ cup chopped fresh cilantro
1 tablespoon olive oil
1 tablespoon fresh lime juice
½ teaspoon table salt
½ teaspoon sugar

Toss together all the ingredients in a large bowl. Cover and chill until ready to serve.

CREAMY DILL SLAW

Adding sour cream lends a mellow richness to this tasty, creamy slaw. The more dill, the better, in my opinion, which is why I add plenty of the chopped fresh herb to the mix, and gild the lily with a bit more sprinkled on top to garnish. Dare I say dill-icious?

SERVES 8 • HANDS-ON: 5 MINUTES • TOTAL: 5 MINUTES, PLUS 8 HOURS CHILLING TIME

4 scallions, sliced
1 (8-ounce) container sour cream
1 cup mayonnaise
2 tablespoons sugar
2 tablespoons chopped fresh dill
2 tablespoons white vinegar
1 teaspoon table salt
½ teaspoon freshly ground black pepper
1 (16-ounce) package shredded coleslaw mix
1 (10-ounce) package finely shredded cabbage
Garnish: chopped fresh dill

Stir together the first 8 ingredients in a large bowl until the mixture is blended; stir in the coleslaw mix and the cabbage. Cover and chill 8 hours. Garnish, if desired.

SAUTÉED GREEN BEANS *with* BACON

Eat your vegetables, and your bacon—that's my idea of having my cake and eating it too. I'll come clean and tell you that I'm the annoying guy at the store who picks green beans one at a time. I like to fill my bag with smaller beans for tender texture and sweeter flavor.

SERVES 4 TO 6 • HANDS-ON: 25 MINUTES • TOTAL: 25 MINUTES

1¾ pounds fresh green beans, trimmed
¼ cup (2 ounces) water
8 bacon slices, chopped
5 scallions (white bottoms and light green parts of tops only), chopped
½ teaspoon table salt
½ teaspoon freshly ground black pepper

1. Place the green beans and ¼ cup water in a large microwave-safe bowl. Cover with plastic wrap, and pierce plastic wrap with a fork. Microwave at HIGH 4 to 7 minutes or until crisp-tender. Plunge the green beans into ice water to stop the cooking process. Drain well.
2. Cook the bacon in a large nonstick skillet over medium until crisp; remove the bacon, and drain on paper towels, reserving 2 tablespoons of the drippings in a small bowl. Discard remaining drippings. Wipe skillet clean with a paper towel.
3. Sauté the scallions in skillet in the hot reserved drippings over medium-high 1 minute. Stir in the green beans, salt, and pepper; sauté 2 to 3 minutes. Stir in the bacon.

SWEET POTATO CORNBREAD

Most diehards will tell you that cornbread should never be sweet. I pity the fools. The addition of sweet potatoes takes this Southern favorite to new heights, creating a scrumptious, moist bread to either sandwich pulled pork or top while still warm with butter.

SERVES 6 • HANDS-ON: 15 MINUTES • TOTAL: 50 MINUTES

2 cups self-rising white cornmeal mix
3 tablespoons sugar
¼ teaspoon pumpkin pie spice
5 large eggs
2 cups mashed cooked sweet potato (about 1½ pounds sweet potato)
1 (8-ounce) container sour cream
4 ounces (½ cup) salted butter, melted

Preheat the oven to 425°F. Lightly grease a 9-inch square pan. Stir together the first 3 ingredients in a large bowl; make a well in center of the mixture. Whisk together the eggs and next 3 ingredients; add to the cornmeal mixture, stirring just until moistened. Spoon the batter into prepared pan, and bake at 425°F for 35 minutes or until golden brown.

Sautéed Green Beans with Bacon

Sweet Potato Cornbread

BACON AND BOURBON COLLARDS

A smart cook always has a stash of bourbon in the kitchen, knowing it is good for cooking, gossip, and keeping the cook hydrated. If the bourbon wasn't enough, these collards also get braised in beer, along with some spice and vinegar to provide the right punch of acidity. I prefer to cook my collards just past al dente, but not to the point where they are a hump of mush. After an hour or so, or in my case, a few bourbons, they should be perfect.

SERVES 10 • HANDS-ON: 40 MINUTES • TOTAL: 1 HOUR, 40 MINUTES

4 thick bacon slices
1½ ounces (3 tablespoons) salted butter
1 large sweet onion, diced
1 (12-ounce) bottle ale
½ cup firmly packed brown sugar
½ cup (4 ounces) bourbon
1 teaspoon red pepper flakes
6 pounds fresh collard greens, trimmed and chopped
½ cup (4 ounces) apple cider vinegar
1 teaspoon table salt
½ teaspoon freshly ground black pepper

1. Cut the bacon crosswise into ¼-inch strips. Melt the butter in a large Dutch oven over medium; add the bacon, and cook, stirring often, 8 minutes or until crisp. Drain the bacon on paper towels, reserving the drippings in skillet. Sauté the onion in the hot drippings 3 minutes or until the onion is tender. Stir in the bacon, ale, and next 3 ingredients; cook 3 minutes or until the mixture is reduced by one-fourth.

2. Add the collards, in batches, and cook, stirring occasionally, 5 minutes or until wilted. Reduce heat to medium-low; cover and cook 1 hour or to desired degree of doneness. Stir in the vinegar, salt, and pepper.

ROOT BEER BAKED BEANS

A cold root beer out of a glass bottle was one of my favorite childhood treats. This dish pays homage to such good memories by transforming canned pork and beans into a dish that's both sweet and savory, with the sweet bite of root beer laced throughout. Did I mention this takes less than five minutes to prep and put into the oven?

SERVES 4 • HANDS-ON: 5 MINUTES • TOTAL: 1 HOUR, 5 MINUTES

3 bacon slices
1 small onion, diced
2 (16-ounce) cans pork and beans
½ cup (4 ounces) root beer
¼ cup (2 ounces) hickory-smoked barbecue sauce
½ teaspoon dry mustard
⅛ teaspoon hot sauce

1. Preheat the oven to 400°F. Lightly grease (with cooking spray) a 1-quart baking dish. Cook the bacon in a skillet over medium until crisp; remove and drain on paper towels, reserving 2 tablespoons drippings in skillet. Crumble the bacon.
2. Sauté the diced onion in the hot bacon drippings in skillet over high 5 minutes or until tender. Stir together the onion, crumbled bacon, beans, and remaining ingredients in prepared baking dish.
3. Bake the beans, uncovered, at 400°F for 55 minutes or until the sauce is thickened.

BARBECUE BEANS

Nothing goes better with a burger or pulled pork sandwich than barbecue baked beans. A little sweet and a little spicy, this delicious side dish will win rave reviews at your next backyard cookout. You can chill the beans eight hours ahead of time if you'd like.

SERVES 10 • HANDS-ON: 25 MINUTES • TOTAL: 1 HOUR, 25 MINUTES

½ medium onion, chopped
½ pound ground beef (optional)
10 bacon slices, cooked and crumbled
⅔ cup firmly packed brown sugar
¾ cup (6 ounces) barbecue sauce
1 (15-ounce) can kidney beans, drained and rinsed
1 (15-ounce) can butter beans, drained and rinsed
1 (15-ounce) can pork and beans
2 tablespoons molasses
2 teaspoons Dijon mustard
½ teaspoon table salt
½ teaspoon freshly ground black pepper
½ teaspoon chili powder

1. Cook onion and, if desired, ground beef in a Dutch oven, stirring until meat crumbles and is no longer pink; drain. Stir in the bacon and remaining ingredients, and spoon into a lightly greased 2½-quart baking dish. Chill 8 hours, if desired.
2. Preheat the oven to 350°F. Bake bean mixture at 350°F for 1 hour, stirring once.

Root Beer Baked Beans

RED BEANS AND RICE

The key to any one-pot dish is cooking everything in one pot, duh. Might sound overly simplistic, but it's all about building flavors and developing them over time. For added spice and authenticity, sub the smoked sausage for a Cajun andouille. Serve over hot cooked white rice . . . and extra props to those who wash it all down with an Abita beer.

SERVES 10 TO 12 • HANDS-ON: 30 MINUTES • TOTAL: 3 HOURS, 55 MINUTES

1 (16-ounce) package dried red kidney beans
1 pound mild smoked sausage, cut into ¼-inch-thick slices
1 (½-pound) smoked ham hock, cut in half
¼ cup vegetable oil
3 celery ribs, diced
1 medium-size yellow onion, diced
1 green bell pepper, diced
3 bay leaves
3 garlic cloves, chopped
2 tablespoons salt-free Cajun seasoning
1 teaspoon kosher salt
1 teaspoon dried thyme
1 teaspoon freshly ground black pepper
3 (32-ounce) containers reduced-sodium chicken broth
Hot cooked rice

1. Place the beans in a large Dutch oven; add water to cover 2 inches above beans. Boil 1 minute; cover, remove from heat, and let stand 1 hour. Drain.
2. Cook the sausage and the ham in hot oil in Dutch oven over medium-high 8 to 10 minutes or until browned. Drain the sausage and the ham on paper towels, reserving 2 tablespoons drippings in skillet. Add the celery and the next 8 ingredients to the drippings; cook over low, stirring occasionally, 15 minutes.
3. Add the broth, beans, sausage, and ham to Dutch oven. Bring to a simmer. Cook, stirring occasionally, 2 hours or until the beans are tender. Discard the ham hock and the bay leaves. Serve over the hot cooked rice.

GRILLED FINGERLING POTATO SALAD

I can't believe that I'm saying this, but I'm serious when I tell you that the bacon is "optional" in this dish. Sounds sacrilegious, but the Pickled Shallots and mustard vinaigrette pack so much punch, you seriously wouldn't miss the bacon. That is, until, you make this dish one day and decide to add bacon. I'll be darned, once you've added that "optional" ingredient, you'll be equally hard pressed to ever go back.

SERVES 8 • HANDS-ON: 20 MINUTES
TOTAL: 3 HOURS, INCLUDING VINAIGRETTE AND PICKLED SHALLOTS

6 cups fingerling potatoes (about 3 pounds), halved lengthwise
2 tablespoons extra virgin olive oil
1 teaspoon kosher salt
½ teaspoon freshly ground black pepper
3 tablespoons Whole-Grain Mustard Vinaigrette (recipe below)
3 tablespoons Pickled Shallots (recipe opposite)
2 tablespoons chopped fresh chives
2 tablespoons chopped fresh flat-leaf parsley
1 teaspoon chopped fresh thyme
3 tablespoons cooked and crumbled bacon (optional)

1. Preheat the grill to 350° to 400°F (medium-high). Toss the potatoes with the olive oil; sprinkle with the salt and pepper. Place the potatoes, cut sides down, on cooking grate; grill, covered with grill lid, 2 minutes or until grill marks appear.
2. Remove from grill. Place the potatoes in a single layer in the center of a large piece of heavy-duty aluminum foil. Bring up foil sides over potatoes; double fold top and side edges to seal, making a packet. Grill the potatoes, in foil packet, covered with grill lid, 15 minutes on each side.
3. Remove packet from grill. Carefully open packet, using tongs. Cool 5 minutes. Toss together the potatoes, vinaigrette, next 4 ingredients, and the bacon, if desired.

WHOLE-GRAIN MUSTARD VINAIGRETTE

¼ cup (2 ounces) white wine vinegar
1 tablespoon light brown sugar
3 tablespoons coarse-grain mustard
½ teaspoon freshly ground black pepper
⅛ teaspoon table salt
⅓ cup olive oil

Whisk together the vinegar, brown sugar, mustard, freshly ground black pepper, and salt. Add the olive oil in a slow, steady stream, whisking constantly until smooth. Makes ⅔ cup

PICKLED SHALLOTS

¾ cup (6 ounces) water
¾ cup (6 ounces) red wine vinegar
⅓ cup sugar
2 tablespoons kosher salt
½ teaspoon red pepper flakes
1½ cups thinly sliced shallots

Bring the water, vinegar, sugar, kosher salt, and red pepper flakes to a boil, whisking until the sugar and salt are dissolved. Pour over the shallots in a sterilized canning jar. Cool to room temperature. Cover and chill 1 hour. Makes 1½ cups

Creamed Corn

CREAMED CORN

This dish highlighting fresh-shucked corn is made even better with some love—cream and butter. Keep an eye on the corn as it simmers; it needs to cook only until it's just tender. If it starts to dry out and stick to the skillet, add a bit more water to loosen the mixture.

SERVES 6 TO 8 • HANDS-ON: 30 MINUTES • TOTAL: 1 HOUR

6 cups fresh corn kernels (from about 13 ears)
¼ to ½ cup (2 to 4 ounces) heavy cream
1 tablespoon unsalted butter
½ teaspoon table salt
⅛ teaspoon freshly ground black pepper
Minced fresh chives (optional)

Cook the corn in a small Dutch oven over low, stirring often, about 30 minutes or until corn is tender. (To prevent the corn from drying out, add up to 10 tablespoons water, 1 tablespoon at a time as needed, during last 15 minutes of cook time.) Stir in the cream and the butter, and cook, stirring occasionally, about 5 minutes or to desired consistency. Stir in the salt and the pepper. Sprinkle with the chives, if desired.

SMOKED CORN

Smoking ears of corn in the husks over wood chips for 30 minutes creates an amazingly rich, smoky flavor. After the corn is smoked, top it with more thyme butter for a fresh herb note.

SERVES 6 TO 8 • HANDS-ON: 15 MINUTES • TOTAL: 1 HOUR, 25 MINUTES

Hickory wood chips
4 ounces (½ cup) salted butter, softened
2 tablespoons chopped fresh thyme
8 ears fresh corn with husks

1. Soak the wood chips in water at least 30 minutes. Prepare charcoal fire in smoker according to manufacturer's instructions; maintain internal temperature at 225° to 235°F for 15 to 20 minutes.
2. Stir together the butter and thyme. Remove heavy outer husks from corn; pull back inner husks. Remove and discard silks. Rub corn with the butter mixture. Pull husks back over corn.
3. Drain chips, and place on coals. Place water pan in smoker; add water to depth of fill line. Place the corn on upper food rack; cover with smoker lid. Smoke 30 to 40 minutes or until corn is tender. Remove the corn from smoker, and let stand 10 minutes. Pull husks back, and serve.

SQUASH CASSEROLE

This beautiful and comforting side dish boasts plenty of summertime's buttery, sweet squash. I like to go a bit old school on this recipe, adding the French fried onions traditionally used atop a green bean casserole. I like the crunch they add to this cheesy baked classic.

SERVES 8 TO 10 • HANDS-ON: 40 MINUTES • TOTAL: 1 HOUR, 15 MINUTES

4 pounds yellow squash, sliced
1 large sweet onion, finely chopped
4 ounces Cheddar cheese, shredded (1 cup)
1 cup mayonnaise
2 tablespoons chopped fresh basil
1 teaspoon garlic salt
1 teaspoon freshly ground black pepper
2 large eggs, lightly beaten
2 cups soft, fresh breadcrumbs
5 ounces Parmesan cheese, grated (1¼ cups)
1 ounce (2 tablespoons) salted butter, melted
½ cup crushed French fried onions
Fresh basil

1. Preheat the oven to 350°F. Lightly grease a 13- x 9-inch baking dish. Cook the yellow squash and the sweet onion in boiling water to cover in a Dutch oven 8 minutes or just until the vegetables are tender; drain the squash mixture well.
2. Combine the squash mixture, freshly shredded Cheddar cheese, next 5 ingredients, 1 cup of the breadcrumbs, and ¾ cup of the Parmesan cheese. Spoon into prepared baking dish.
3. Stir together the melted butter, French fried onions, and remaining 1 cup breadcrumbs and ½ cup Parmesan cheese. Sprinkle over the squash mixture.
4. Bake at 350°F for 35 to 40 minutes or until set. Garnish with additional fresh basil.

MEATY MAINS

CHICKEN BRUNSWICK STEW

Brunswick stew is a hearty, Southern-style stew that's packed full of meat and veggies and has a slightly sweet flavor from either chili sauce or ketchup. The original Brunswick stew was made with squirrel meat, but this slow-cooker version features shredded chicken.

SERVES 6 • HANDS-ON: 20 MINUTES • TOTAL: 5 HOURS, 20 MINUTES

2 large onions, chopped
6 boneless, skinless chicken breasts
2 (15-ounce) cans cream-style corn
1 (28-ounce) can crushed tomatoes
1 (12-ounce) bottle chili sauce
1 (14-ounce) can chicken broth
¼ cup (2 ounces) Worcestershire sauce
2 ounces (¼ cup) salted butter, cut up
2 tablespoons apple cider vinegar
2 teaspoons dry mustard
½ teaspoon table salt
½ teaspoon freshly ground black pepper
½ teaspoon pepper sauce

Place onion in a 4-quart slow cooker; place chicken over onion. Add corn and remaining ingredients. Cover and cook on HIGH 5 hours or until chicken is tender. Remove chicken; shred and return to stew.

SUMMER BRUNSWICK STEW

Why wait for the first frost to enjoy this Georgia-inspired classic stew? I like to take advantage of the fresh summer produce to make a lightened up version of this comfort dish. My preference is to go with a thin, vinegar-based BBQ sauce whenever possible—adding in just a bit at a time until I get that slightly sweet-and-sour taste that keeps my spoon moving from bowl to mouth.

SERVES 10 • HANDS-ON: 20 MINUTES • TOTAL: 50 MINUTES

1 large sweet onion, diced
2 tablespoons olive oil
2 garlic cloves, minced
6 cups (48 ounces) chicken broth
2 cups fresh lady peas or butter peas
1 pound pulled pork (without sauce)
1 pound Yukon gold potatoes, peeled and diced (about 2 cups)
2 cups fresh corn kernels (about 4 ears)
1 to 1½ cups (8 to 12 ounces) barbecue sauce
2 cups peeled and diced tomatoes
Table salt and freshly ground black pepper

Sauté the onion in hot oil in a Dutch oven over medium 5 minutes or until tender; add the garlic, and sauté 1 minute. Add the broth and the peas; bring to a boil, stirring often. Cover, reduce heat to medium-low, and simmer, stirring occasionally, 15 minutes or until the peas are tender. Stir in the pork and next 3 ingredients; cover and simmer, stirring occasionally, 15 minutes or until the potatoes are tender. Add the tomatoes, and season with salt and pepper to taste.

Smoked
Brisket Pho

Pork Belly Tonkatsu Ramen

PORK BELLY TONKATSU RAMEN

Authentic Japanese ramen seems to be all the rage these days. Trust me—this stuff is way different from that cup o' noodle concoction that first comes to mind during the good ole college years. Truth be told, an authentic Tonkatsu broth typically takes several days to brew and stew—producing a creamy, fatty broth that is transcending. To save time, I've married bacon and mushrooms together, along with a store-bought stock that produces a legitimate shortcut replication. To make things even better, I've topped it all off with a soft-boiled egg and smoked pork belly. Bring on the food coma.

SERVES 4 • HANDS-ON: 20 MINUTES • TOTAL: 40 MINUTES

5 cups (40 ounces) chicken broth
8 ounces thick-cut bacon slices (about 8 slices)
1 ounce dried shiitake mushrooms
2 tablespoons soy sauce
4 large eggs
1 small bunch fresh collard greens, stems removed and leaves thinly sliced (about 3 cups)
8 ounces uncooked Chinese egg noodles, prepared according to package directions
8 ounces Smoked Pork Belly (page 194), sliced
¼ cup thinly sliced scallions

1. Stir together the broth, bacon, and shiitake mushrooms in a large saucepan over medium-high; cover and bring to a boil. Remove pan from heat, and let stand, covered, 20 minutes. Pour the mixture through a wire-mesh strainer into a bowl; discard solids. Return the broth to pan; stir in the soy sauce, and keep warm.

2. Add water to a Dutch oven to a depth of 1 inch, and bring to a simmer over high. Set a steamer basket in Dutch oven. Add the eggs to steamer basket, and reduce heat to medium-low. Cover and steam the eggs 6 minutes. Add the collards to steamer basket; cover and steam 2 minutes. Remove the collards. Transfer the eggs to a bowl of ice water, and let stand until slightly cool, about 1 minute. Peel the eggs, and cut in half lengthwise.

3. Divide the noodles evenly among 4 deep bowls; top with the collards and the pork belly. Ladle 1 cup warm broth into each bowl. Place 2 egg halves in each bowl; sprinkle with the scallions, and serve immediately.

SMOKED BRISKET PHO

I like to think that if you put classic, Texas-style brisket on an airplane to Vietnam, it would end up as the star topping in their classic dish, pho. Pho, a clear-based noodle soup brimming with savory aromatics, is typically served with thinly sliced raw beef—the steaming hot broth just cooks the beef up to temperature. In this method, we take perfectly smoked brisket (leftover brisket is also a great option) and serve it as a topping with crispy bean sprouts, basil, lime, and chiles. East meets West meets Delicious.

SERVES 4 • HANDS-ON: 15 MINUTES • TOTAL: 35 MINUTES

2 teaspoons canola oil
1 large yellow onion, sliced
1 (2-inch) piece peeled fresh ginger, sliced
2 garlic cloves, smashed
5 cups (40 ounces) beef consommé
1 whole star anise
1 whole clove
1 (3-inch) cinnamon stick
2 tablespoons fish sauce
2 tablespoons fresh lime juice
1 teaspoon granulated sugar
¼ teaspoon freshly ground black pepper
8 ounces uncooked flat rice noodles (banh pho), prepared according to package directions
¾ pound sliced smoked brisket (such as B-Daddy's Brisket, page 143)
1 cup fresh bean sprouts
¼ cup loosely packed fresh basil leaves, torn
2 red or green jalapeño chiles, seeded and thinly sliced
¼ cup prepared barbecue sauce (such as Sweet BBQ Sauce, page 30)
Lime wedges
Garnish: fresh basil

1. Heat the oil in a heavy saucepan over medium-high. Add the onion, ginger, and garlic, and cook, stirring often, until lightly browned, about 6 minutes. Add the consommé, star anise, clove, and cinnamon stick. Bring to a boil; reduce heat to medium-low, and simmer, stirring occasionally, 15 minutes. Pour the mixture through a wire-mesh strainer into a bowl; discard solids. Return the broth to pan; stir in the fish sauce, lime juice, sugar, and black pepper.
2. Divide the noodles evenly among 4 deep bowls; top with the brisket and bean sprouts. Ladle 1 cup warm broth into each bowl. Top with the basil and the jalapeño slices, and serve immediately with the barbecue sauce and the lime wedges. Garnish, if desired.

SMOKED PIZZA *with* PULLED PORK

If you are not hip to grilling pizzas, now is the time to get with it. The direct heat from the grill turns out a restaurant-quality, crispy crust—you'd never get the same results in an oven. I've taken it one step further in this recipe, by tossing in some wood chips to add even more smoke flavor. I've provided some of my favorite pizza toppings, but this grilling method can be used to produce a pizza with nearly any topping imaginable. The best part? This recipe comes together quite quickly—making it the perfect meal for a busy weeknight.

SERVES 4 • HANDS-ON: 20 MINUTES • TOTAL: 55 MINUTES

Barbecue Sauce
1½ cups (12 ounces) ketchup
¼ cup (2 ounces) apple cider vinegar
1 tablespoon freshly ground black pepper
1 tablespoon spicy brown mustard
1½ teaspoons light brown sugar
1 teaspoon kosher salt
1 teaspoon minced garlic

Pizza
Parchment paper
1 pound fresh deli pizza dough
3 cups applewood chips (do not soak)
1 pound pulled pork (without sauce), chopped
½ cup thinly sliced red onion (about 1 small onion)
2 ounces mozzarella cheese, shredded (about ½ cup)
2 ounces Gruyère cheese, shredded (about ½ cup)

1. Make the Barbecue Sauce: Stir together the ketchup, vinegar, pepper, mustard, brown sugar, salt, and garlic in a saucepan over medium-high; bring to a boil. Reduce heat to low, and simmer, stirring occasionally, 10 minutes. Remove from heat.

2. Make the Pizza: Lightly grease (with cooking spray) a sheet of parchment paper. Place the pizza dough on a lightly floured surface, and cover with plastic wrap. Let stand 30 minutes. Roll dough into about a 12-inch round. Transfer dough round to prepared parchment paper.

3. Place a large pizza stone on grate on 1 side of a gas grill. Preheat both sides of grill to medium (about 350°F). Tear or cut 1 (18-inch) square of heavy-duty aluminum foil; place the applewood chips in center. Fold foil to enclose chips, and pierce several holes in packet. Place foil packet on grate on other lit side of grill.

4. Carefully transfer the dough to hot pizza stone. Turn off side of grill with foil packet. Grill, covered with grill lid, until the pizza dough is golden brown, 4 to 6 minutes. Carefully turn the crust over, and spread with 1 cup of the sauce. Top with the pulled pork, onion, and cheeses, and grill, covered with grill lid, until the cheeses are browned and bubbly, 3 to 4 minutes. Cut the pizza into 8 slices, and serve with remaining ½ cup sauce for dipping.

BBQ PORK QUESADILLAS

Everybody chant after me: snacks, Snacks, SNACKS! This easy recipe is one of my go-to's when I have leftover pork on hand. A cast-iron pan produces the best result—its heavy bottom ensures an even temperature—so the cheese is melted without burning the tortilla.

SERVES 4 • HANDS-ON: 25 MINUTES • TOTAL: 25 MINUTES

1 pound pulled pork (without sauce)
1 cup (8 ounces) barbecue sauce
½ cup chopped fresh cilantro
2 scallions, minced
8 (6-inch) fajita-size flour tortillas
1 (8-ounce) package shredded Mexican 4-cheese blend
Toppings: sour cream, sliced scallions, chopped fresh cilantro, barbecue sauce

1. Stir together the pork and next 3 ingredients.
2. Lightly grease a skillet or griddle. Place 1 tortilla in prepared skillet or on griddle. Sprinkle the tortilla with ¼ cup cheese, and spoon ⅓ cup pork mixture on half of the tortilla. Cook 2 to 3 minutes or until the cheese melts. Fold the tortilla in half over the filling; transfer to a serving plate. Repeat procedure with remaining tortillas, cheese, and pork mixture. Serve with the desired toppings.

BBQ TORTILLA PIE

My favorite snack at the ballpark was a good ole Frito pie. I go more "adult" here, adding a slew of toppings to satisfy nearly any appetite. I find that this casual supper is also great for entertaining—it's unpretentious and delicious. Feel free to add extra items your family or friends enjoy such as corn, chopped bell pepper, avocado, or sliced jalapeño chiles.

SERVES 4 TO 6 • HANDS-ON: 15 MINUTES • TOTAL: 15 MINUTES

1 (3.5-ounce) package boil-in-bag rice
1 tablespoon chopped fresh cilantro (optional)
1 (15-ounce) bag corn chips
5 to 6 cups pulled pork or shredded brisket (without sauce)
½ head iceberg lettuce, shredded, or 1 (10-ounce) package shredded iceberg lettuce
1 (8-ounce) package shredded Cheddar-Jack cheese blend
3 plum tomatoes, chopped
4 scallions, chopped
Sour cream
1 (2.25-ounce) can sliced ripe black olives, drained (optional)
1 (12-ounce) jar pickled jalapeño chiles (optional)

1. Prepare the rice according to package directions. Stir in the cilantro, if desired.
2. Layer the rice mixture, chips, pork or brisket, next 5 ingredients, and if desired, the black olives and jalapeño chiles in individual serving bowls.

BBQ Pork
Quesadillas

BBQ Tortilla Pie

Easy Barbecue Tostadas

EASY BARBECUE TOSTADAS

A tostada serves as a nice change of pace from taco night. Essentially a flat, crispy shell, a tostada functions as a blank canvas for nearly any topping. Make your life even easier and use leftover or store-bought rotisserie chicken or pulled pork along with your favorite toppings.

SERVES 10 • HANDS-ON: 30 MINUTES
TOTAL: 45 MINUTES, INCLUDING SAUCE, CREAM, AND SLAW

1 (16-ounce) can refried beans
10 tostada shells
2 pounds pulled pork or chicken (without sauce)
Mole Barbecue Sauce (recipe below)
Chipotle Sour Cream (recipe below)
Jicama Slaw (page 207)

Spread refried beans evenly on the tostada shells. Top with the pulled pork or chicken, Mole Barbecue Sauce, Chipotle Sour Cream, and Jicama Slaw. Serve immediately.

MOLE BARBECUE SAUCE

It's the bittersweet dark chocolate in the mole sauce that transforms this traditional BBQ sauce into a condiment with incredible depth and complexity in every bite.

1 tablespoon mole sauce
¼ cup (2 ounces) hot water
1 cup (8 ounces) barbecue sauce
1 tablespoon fresh lime juice
1 tablespoon chopped fresh cilantro

Whisk together the mole sauce and the hot water until smooth. Whisk in the barbecue sauce, lime juice, and chopped fresh cilantro. Makes about 1½ cups

CHIPOTLE SOUR CREAM

½ cup sour cream
1 chipotle pepper in adobo sauce, minced
Pinch of table salt

Stir together the sour cream, minced chipotle pepper, and salt. Makes ½ cup

Brisket Tacos

Redneck Tacos

REDNECK TACOS

You might be a redneck if . . . kidding! Trust me, these tacos ain't your average quick fix. What really sets these guys apart is the homemade corn cakes. If you've never been brave enough to try these at home, drink a cold beer, fire up the stove, and give them a try. Finished with your favorite pulled pork, sauce, and queso, this recipe will ensure that taco night is anything but average.

SERVES 6 • HANDS-ON: 35 MINUTES • TOTAL: 1 HOUR, 40 MINUTES, INCLUDING SAUCES

2 cups stone-ground yellow cornmeal
1 teaspoon ground cumin
1 teaspoon baking soda
2 teaspoons kosher salt
1 cup (8 ounces) whole buttermilk
1 large egg, lightly beaten
¼ cup plus 2 tablespoons canola oil
1 scallion, thinly sliced
⅓ cup (about 3 ounces) apple cider vinegar
1 teaspoon ancho chile powder
1 teaspoon granulated sugar
½ small head savoy cabbage, shredded or finely chopped
1 jalapeño chile, seeded and thinly sliced
½ cup grated carrot
2 tablespoons chopped fresh cilantro
¼ teaspoon freshly ground black pepper
1½ pounds pulled pork, warmed
2 ounces queso fresco, crumbled (about ½ cup)
White BBQ Sauce (page 32)
Sweet BBQ Sauce (page 30)
Lime wedges

1. Stir together the cornmeal, cumin, baking soda, and 1 teaspoon of the salt in a medium bowl. Stir together the buttermilk, egg, and 2 tablespoons of the oil; stir into the cornmeal mixture just until blended. Stir in the scallions.
2. Brush 1 tablespoon of the oil on the bottom of a 12-inch cast-iron skillet, and heat over medium-high. Drop the cornmeal mixture in ¼ cupfuls into hot skillet. Flatten to ½-inch thickness, and cook, about 3 cakes at a time, until golden, 1½ to 2 minutes on each side. Repeat process with remaining batter and oil. Keep the corn cakes warm in a 200°F oven, if desired.
3. Whisk together the vinegar, chile powder, and sugar in a large bowl. Add the cabbage, jalapeño, carrot, and cilantro, and toss to coat. Sprinkle with the black pepper and remaining 1 teaspoon salt, and let stand 15 minutes before serving, tossing occasionally.
4. Top the corn cakes with the pulled pork, slaw, and queso fresco. Drizzle with White and Sweet Barbecue Sauce. Serve with the lime wedges.

BRISKET TACOS

In my home, Sundays are reserved for church, family, and slow cooking. Instead of heating up my whole house by turning on the oven (it's hot in the South, remember), I like to allow my slow cooker to do most of the work—producing an exceptionally moist, tender brisket. Pile these tacos high with your favorite toppings, and chalk this stress-free meal up to another Sunday Funday.

SERVES 6 TO 8 • HANDS-ON: 30 MINUTES • TOTAL: 7 HOURS, 30 MINUTES

2 bacon slices, cut into 1-inch pieces
1 medium-size white onion, chopped (about 1 cup)
2 teaspoons kosher salt
1 teaspoon freshly ground black pepper
1 (3- to 3½-pound) beef brisket, trimmed
1 cup (8 ounces) reduced-sodium chicken broth
3 canned chipotle peppers in adobo sauce
3 tablespoons adobo sauce from can
3 garlic cloves, peeled and smashed
1 tablespoon ground cumin
1 tablespoon Worcestershire sauce
1 tablespoon honey
1 teaspoon dried oregano
2 tablespoons apple cider vinegar
10 to 12 (8-inch) flour tortillas, warmed
Crunchy Summer Salsa (page 278) (optional)

1. Place the bacon and onion in a 6- to 8-quart slow cooker. Stir together the salt and pepper; sprinkle over all sides of the brisket. Place the brisket in slow cooker.
2. Process the broth and next 7 ingredients in a blender for 30 seconds or until smooth; pour the mixture over the brisket. Cover and cook on LOW 7 hours or until the brisket is fork-tender. Transfer the brisket to a 13- x 9-inch baking dish; cover with aluminum foil to keep warm.
3. Pour the sauce through a fine wire-mesh strainer into a medium saucepan, and cook over medium-high, stirring occasionally, 15 to 20 minutes or until reduced to ⅓ cup. Stir in the vinegar.
4. Coarsely chop the brisket; spoon over the warm tortillas. Drizzle with the sauce. Serve with Crunchy Summer Salsa, if desired.

BBQ SPAGHETTI

A staple of Memphis, Tennessee, BBQ Spaghetti is one of my family's favorite meals. In fact, I often find myself making this as a "stretch" meal when I've reserved some pork from a weekend cookout. Pro tip: I highly encourage you to top this bowl of pork and noodles with an amount of finely shredded Cheddar cheese to the point that it seems unreasonable. Try it, and you'll get my gist.

SERVES 6 • HANDS-ON: 12 MINUTES • TOTAL: 1 HOUR, 55 MINUTES

2 cups (16 ounces) ketchup
1 cup (8 ounces) chicken broth
½ cup (4 ounces) apple cider vinegar
2 tablespoons light brown sugar
2 tablespoons fresh lemon juice
2 tablespoons Worcestershire sauce
1½ teaspoons onion powder
1½ teaspoons dry mustard
1½ teaspoons kosher salt
½ teaspoon freshly ground black pepper
2 tablespoons extra virgin olive oil
1 cup chopped green bell pepper (about 1 medium pepper)
1 medium-size yellow onion, diced
3 garlic cloves, minced
1½ pounds pulled pork
1 pound hot cooked spaghetti
2 ounces Cheddar cheese, shredded (about ½ cup)
¼ cup coarsely chopped fresh flat-leaf parsley

1. Stir together the ketchup, broth, vinegar, brown sugar, lemon juice, Worcestershire sauce, onion powder, and dry mustard in a small Dutch oven over medium-high. Bring to a boil, stirring occasionally. Reduce heat to low; stir in the salt and pepper, and simmer, stirring occasionally, 1 hour.
2. Heat the oil in a medium skillet over medium-high. Add the bell pepper and onion, and cook, stirring often, until the vegetables soften, about 5 minutes. Stir in the garlic, and cook, stirring often, 1 minute. Stir the vegetable mixture and the pulled pork into the sauce in the Dutch oven, and simmer, stirring occasionally, about 40 minutes.
3. Divide the cooked spaghetti evenly among 6 bowls. Spoon the pulled pork sauce over the spaghetti, and sprinkle with the cheese and the parsley.

DOWN-SOUTH BANH MI

I'm a big believer that a good sandwich is suitable and entirely appropriate when served for supper. Take this one, for example—a Southern spin on a classic Vietnamese-French sub. I like to make a big batch of the pickled pepper mixture—ensuring I can consume as much as I want for a snack, or of course, as a topping for this delicious sandwich when the craving strikes!

SERVES 3 • HANDS-ON: 30 MINUTES
TOTAL: 1 HOUR, 30 MINUTES, INCLUDING PEPPERS AND ONIONS

1 (18-inch) French bread baguette
3 tablespoons mayonnaise
1 teaspoon Sriracha chili sauce
¼ cup thinly sliced carrots
1 teaspoon fish sauce
1 cup pulled pork (without sauce)
⅓ cup Pickled Peppers and Onions (recipe below)
1 small serrano or jalapeño chile, thinly sliced
Fresh cilantro leaves

1. Preheat the oven to 350°F. Bake the baguette on an ungreased baking sheet 10 minutes or until warm.
2. Meanwhile, stir together the mayonnaise and Sriracha in a small bowl. Stir together the carrots and the fish sauce in a separate small bowl.
3. Split the baguette horizontally. Cut each half into 3 (6-inch-long) pieces. Spread cut sides of bread with mayonnaise mixture. Layer bottom halves with the pulled pork, Pickled Peppers and Onions, serrano chile slices, carrot mixture, and cilantro to taste. Top with remaining bread slices. Serve immediately.

PICKLED PEPPERS AND ONIONS

½ small red onion, cut into ¼-inch-thick slices
Ice water
½ red bell pepper, cut lengthwise into ¼-inch-wide strips
½ yellow bell pepper, cut lengthwise into ¼-inch-wide strips
½ green bell pepper, cut lengthwise into ¼-inch-wide strips
1 cup (8 ounces) white vinegar
6 tablespoons sugar
2 tablespoons kosher salt
½ teaspoon red pepper flakes
1 cup (8 ounces) water

1. Soak the onion slices in ice water to cover in a small bowl 10 minutes; drain. Place the onion slices and the bell pepper strips in 1 (1-quart) canning jar.
2. Bring the vinegar, next 3 ingredients, and 1 cup water to a boil in a small nonaluminum saucepan over medium-high, stirring occasionally, until sugar is dissolved.
3. Pour the hot vinegar mixture over the vegetables in jar. Let stand, uncovered, 1 hour. Makes 1 quart

SOUTHERN-STYLE CUBAN SANDWICHES

Nothing beats the "scooped out" method of pulling the soft center portion from the bread (feed it to the birds). Not only does it save on calories, it also makes the sandwich all about the delicious pork—and less about the bread.

SERVES 4 TO 6 • HANDS-ON: 20 MINUTES • TOTAL: 30 MINUTES, INCLUDING SAUCE

1 (12-ounce) French bread loaf
Chipotle Rémoulade (recipe below)
1 pound sliced smoked pork (without sauce)
4 (1-ounce) provolone cheese slices
1 cup sweet-hot pickles

1. Cut the French bread loaf in half horizontally; scoop out the soft bread from center of each half, leaving a ½-inch-thick border. (Reserve the soft bread for another use.)
2. Spread the inside of bread shells with the Chipotle Rémoulade. Layer the bottom shell with the smoked pork, provolone cheese slices, and sweet-hot pickles. Top with remaining bread shell. Cut into individual sandwiches.

CHIPOTLE RÉMOULADE

Traditionally, rémoulade is a mayo- and mustard-based sauce used as a condiment throughout Cajun country. But why limit this zesty condiment to just one region? A bit of canned chipotle pepper and its adobo sauce creates a sauce with new intensity and flavor.

¾ cup mayonnaise
2 tablespoons Creole mustard
2 tablespoons sweet-hot pickle relish
1 canned chipotle pepper in adobo sauce, chopped
1 tablespoon chopped fresh flat-leaf parsley
½ teaspoon lemon zest
2 teaspoons fresh lemon juice
⅛ teaspoon table salt
⅛ teaspoon freshly ground black pepper

Stir together the mayonnaise, Creole mustard, pickle relish, chopped chipotle pepper, parsley, lemon zest, lemon juice, salt, and pepper in a small bowl. Cover and chill up to 3 days before serving. Makes 1 cup

BARBECUE POT PIE *with* CHEESE GRITS CRUST

. . . aka "comfort cooking on a winter night." For me, this dish screams "eat me on the couch, glass of red wine in hand, under a blanket, and with a good holiday movie on the tube." The cheese grits crust can be repurposed sans the pork, turning out a fantastic baked grits dish to serve as a hearty side for any main—regardless of the season.

SERVES 8 TO 10 • HANDS-ON: 25 MINUTES • TOTAL: 45 MINUTES, INCLUDING CRUST

1 large sweet onion, diced
1 tablespoon vegetable oil
2 tablespoons all-purpose flour
1½ cups (12 ounces) thick barbecue sauce
1½ cups (12 ounces) beef broth
1 pound pulled pork or brisket
Cheese Grits Crust Batter (recipe below)

1. Preheat the oven to 425°F. Lightly grease a 13- x 9-inch baking dish or 8 to 10 ramekins. Sauté the onion in hot oil in a large skillet over medium-high 5 minutes or until golden brown. Stir in the flour, and cook, stirring constantly, 1 minute. Gradually stir in the barbecue sauce and the beef broth; cook, stirring constantly, 3 minutes or until the mixture begins to thicken.
2. Stir in the pork, and bring to a boil. Remove from heat, and spoon the mixture into prepared baking dish.
3. Spoon the Cheese Grits Crust Batter evenly over the hot barbecue mixture.
4. Bake at 425°F for 20 to 25 minutes or until golden brown and set.

CHEESE GRITS CRUST BATTER

2 cups (16 ounces) water
2 cups (16 ounces) whole milk
1 cup quick-cooking grits
8 ounces sharp Cheddar cheese, shredded (2 cups)
¾ teaspoon table salt
½ teaspoon seasoned pepper
2 large eggs, lightly beaten

1. Bring the water and the milk to a boil in a large saucepan; add the grits, and cook, stirring often, 5 minutes or until thickened. Stir in the cheese, salt, and pepper; remove from heat.
2. Stir about one-fourth of the hot grits mixture gradually into the beaten eggs; add to remaining hot grits mixture, stirring constantly. Makes 1 (13- x 9-inch) crust or 8 to 10 individual crusts

BEER-CAN STICKY CHICKEN

The day you decide to roast a whole chicken stuffed with beer—that, my friends, is a day of celebration. I like to use a Cajun-inspired dry rub on the bird, finishing the whole kit and caboodle with a sweet, Asian-style BBQ sauce that puts the "stick" in sticky. I've called for a brown ale, but truth be told, any beer will do the trick—at least that's my motto—and I'm sticking to it!

SERVES 8 • HANDS-ON: 15 MINUTES • TOTAL: 1 HOUR, 55 MINUTES, INCLUDING SAUCE

2 tablespoons kosher salt
1 tablespoon light brown sugar
2 teaspoons paprika
1 teaspoon freshly ground black pepper
1 teaspoon dried thyme
1 teaspoon dried oregano
½ teaspoon cayenne pepper
2 (3½- to 4-pound) whole chickens, rinsed and patted dry
2 (12-ounce) cans brown ale
Honey-Soy BBQ Sauce (recipe below)

1. Heat 1 side of a gas grill to medium-high (350° to 400°F); leave other side unlit. Stir together the salt, sugar, paprika, black pepper, thyme, oregano, and cayenne pepper; sprinkle the mixture inside cavity and on outside of each chicken.
2. Reserve ¾ cup of the beer from each for the Honey-Soy BBQ Sauce. Place each chicken upright onto a beer can, fitting can into cavity. Pull the legs forward to form a tripod, so the chicken stands upright.
3. Place the chickens upright on unlit side of grill. Grill, covered with grill lid, rotating the chickens occasionally, until golden and a meat thermometer inserted in thickest portion registers 165°F, 1 hour to 1 hour and 10 minutes. Let stand 10 minutes. Remove the chickens from cans, and slice. Serve with the Honey-Soy BBQ Sauce.

HONEY-SOY BBQ SAUCE

1 cup (8 ounces) ketchup
1½ cups (12 ounces) reserved brown ale
½ cup honey
¼ cup (2 ounces) soy sauce
¼ cup (2 ounces) apple cider vinegar
2 teaspoons garlic powder
½ teaspoon red pepper flakes

Stir together all the ingredients in a medium saucepan over high; bring to a boil. Reduce heat to medium, and cook, stirring occasionally, 30 to 40 minutes or until reduced to about 1½ cups. Makes 1½ cups

PULLED PORK MEXICAN LASAGNA

I have a regular habit of always smoking too much pork—something my friends love about me when I make the rounds in Nashville, handing out pounds of pulled pork to those in hungry anticipation. But sometimes, those friends get pushed to the side. Such is the case with this recipe, as I repurpose my delicious smoked pork with some inspiration from the Southwest—churning out a "lasagna" of sorts that packs tons of flavor into every bite. Ok, ok . . . I don't typically leave my friends hanging, I promise. All are welcome, for the price of a cold beer or two, to pull up a seat at my family table and help me devour this delicious dish.

SERVES 8 • HANDS-ON: 20 MINUTES • TOTAL: 1 HOUR

2 tablespoons olive oil
2 cups fresh corn kernels (from 3 ears)
½ cup chopped white onion (from 1 small onion)
2 garlic cloves, minced
1 pound pulled pork, chopped
1 (15-ounce) can tomato sauce
¾ cup (6 ounces) picante sauce
¼ cup barbecue sauce
1 tablespoon chili powder
1½ teaspoons ground cumin
1 (24-ounce) container 1% low-fat small-curd cottage cheese
2 large eggs, lightly beaten
1 ounce Parmesan cheese, grated (¼ cup)
1 teaspoon dried oregano
12 (5-inch) corn tortillas
4 ounces mild Cheddar cheese, shredded (about 1 cup)
¼ cup chopped fresh cilantro

1. Preheat the oven to 375°F. Lightly grease (with cooking spray) a 13- x 9-inch baking dish. Heat the oil in a large skillet over medium; add the corn, onion, and garlic, and cook, stirring occasionally, until tender, about 5 minutes. Stir in the pork, tomato sauce, picante sauce, barbecue sauce, chili powder, and cumin; bring to a boil. Reduce heat to medium-low, and simmer, stirring often, 5 minutes. Remove from heat.
2. Stir together the cottage cheese, eggs, Parmesan cheese, and oregano in a medium bowl. Arrange 6 of the tortillas on bottom and about 1½ inches up sides of prepared baking dish. Spoon half of the meat mixture over the tortillas; top with the cottage cheese mixture. Arrange remaining 6 tortillas over cottage cheese mixture; top with remaining meat mixture.
3. Bake at 375°F for 30 minutes or until thoroughly heated and bubbly. Remove from oven; sprinkle with the Cheddar cheese, and let stand 10 minutes. Sprinkle with the cilantro just before serving.

BURNT ENDS MAC 'N' CHEESE

Any true connoisseur will often tell you that it's the "butcher's" cuts, often known as the cook's portion, that are always the best. The crowd can have a filet mignon—I'll be just fine with my skirt steak instead. Such is the case with the charred ends of a brisket—one of the most delicious pieces of the cut, yet sometimes discarded because they become a bit tougher and drier than the juicy center. Do not discard! All they need is a little love to bring them back to life, and I like to mix this chopped beef into a homemade creamy, crunchy mac 'n' cheese. Life is good.

SERVES 10 • HANDS-ON: 25 MINUTES • TOTAL: 30 MINUTES

4 quarts water
¼ cup plus 1½ teaspoons kosher salt
1 quart (32 ounces) whole milk
3 ounces (6 tablespoons) salted butter, cut into pieces
6 tablespoons all-purpose flour
8 ounces extra-sharp Cheddar cheese, shredded (about 2 cups)
8 ounces Monterey Jack cheese, shredded (about 2 cups)
1 teaspoon hot sauce (such as Tabasco)
½ teaspoon freshly ground black pepper
1 pound uncooked penne, cavatappi, or rotini pasta
1 pound burnt (or charred) ends smoked brisket (without sauce), chopped
1½ cups panko (Japanese-style breadcrumbs)
2 teaspoons olive oil
½ cup barbecue sauce, warmed
¼ cup thinly sliced fresh chives

1. Preheat the broiler with oven rack 8 to 9 inches from heat. Bring the water and ¼ cup of the salt to a boil in a large Dutch oven, covered, over high.
2. Meanwhile, place the milk in a 1-quart microwave-safe glass measuring cup; cover with plastic wrap, and microwave on HIGH 3 minutes. Melt the butter in a 12-inch cast-iron skillet over medium. Reduce heat to medium-low; add the flour, and cook, whisking constantly, 2 minutes. Gradually whisk in the hot milk. Increase heat to medium, and bring to a low boil, whisking often. Cook, whisking often, 6 minutes. Remove skillet from heat; whisk in the cheeses, hot sauce, pepper, and remaining 1½ teaspoons salt, whisking until blended and smooth. Cover to keep warm.
3. Add the pasta to boiling salted water, and cook 8 minutes. Drain the pasta; fold into the cheese sauce in skillet. Stir in the brisket. Stir together the panko and the olive oil in a small bowl; sprinkle over the mixture in skillet.
4. Broil 1 to 2 minutes or until the panko is golden brown. Drizzle with the barbecue sauce; sprinkle with the chives, and serve immediately.

LA COCOTTE
SWEET
THINGS

BLACKBERRY COBBLER

Aside from the fresh blackberries, this recipe calls for only five additional ingredients—making it an effortless and affordable dish. Class it up a notch by adding a garnish of Chantilly Cream, fresh mint, and lemon zest curls.

SERVES 6 • HANDS-ON: 15 MINUTES • TOTAL: 1 HOUR

4 cups fresh blackberries
1 tablespoon fresh lemon juice
1 large egg
1 cup sugar
1 cup all-purpose flour
3 ounces (6 tablespoons) salted butter, melted
Chantilly Cream (recipe below)
Fresh mint sprigs, lemon zest

1. Preheat the oven to 375°F. Lightly grease an 8-inch square baking dish or 6 (8-ounce) ramekins. Place the blackberries in prepared baking dish; sprinkle with the lemon juice.
2. Stir together the egg, sugar, and flour in a medium bowl until mixture is crumbly. Sprinkle over the fruit. Drizzle the melted butter over the topping.
3. Bake at 375°F for 35 minutes or until lightly browned and bubbly. Let stand 10 minutes. Serve warm with the Chantilly Cream. Garnish with the mint and lemon zest.

CHANTILLY CREAM

1 (8-ounce) container crème fraîche or sour cream
¾ cup (6 ounces) whipping cream
¾ teaspoon vanilla extract
3 tablespoons powdered sugar

Beat the crème fraîche in a large bowl at medium speed with an electric mixer 30 seconds. Add remaining ingredients; beat at high speed 3 minutes or until soft peaks form. Makes about 2 cups

EASY PEACH COBBLER

Growing up in Georgia, I remember peach cobbler was always a constant dessert after supper. A good cobbler shouldn't be too difficult to put together, and this simple recipe ensures that your family can enjoy a sweet finish to nearly any summertime meal.

SERVES 10 • HANDS-ON: 30 MINUTES
TOTAL: 2 HOURS, 45 MINUTES, INCLUDING ICE CREAM, PLUS 8 HOURS CHILLING TIME

4 ounces (½ cup) unsalted butter
1 cup all-purpose flour
2 cups sugar
1 tablespoon baking powder
Pinch of table salt
1 cup (8 ounces) whole milk
4 cups fresh peach slices
1 tablespoon fresh lemon juice
Ground cinnamon or nutmeg (optional)
Vanilla Ice Cream (optional) (recipe below)

1. Preheat the oven to 375°F. Melt the butter in a 13- x 9-inch baking dish.
2. Combine the flour, 1 cup of the sugar, baking powder, and salt; add the milk, stirring just until dry ingredients are moistened. Pour the batter over the butter (do not stir).
3. Bring remaining 1 cup sugar, peach slices, and lemon juice to a boil over high, stirring constantly; pour over the batter (do not stir). Sprinkle with the cinnamon, if desired.
4. Bake at 375°F for 40 to 45 minutes or until golden brown. Serve cobbler warm or cool with ice cream, if desired.

VANILLA ICE CREAM

¾ cup sugar
2 tablespoons cornstarch
⅛ teaspoon table salt
2 cups (16 ounces) whole milk
1 cup (8 ounces) heavy whipping cream
1 large egg yolk
1½ teaspoons vanilla exract

1. Whisk together the first 3 ingredients in a large heavy saucepan. Gradually whisk in the milk and cream. Cook over medium, stirring constantly, 10 to 12 minutes or until mixture thickens slightly. Remove from heat.
2. Whisk the egg yolk until slightly thickened. Gradually whisk about 1 cup of the hot cream mixture into the yolk. Add the yolk mixture to remaining hot cream mixture, whisking constantly. Whisk in the vanilla. Cool 1 hour, stirring occasionally.
3. Place plastic wrap directly on cream mixture, and chill 8 to 24 hours.
4. Pour the mixture into freezer container of a 1½-quart electric ice-cream maker, and freeze according to manufacturer's instructions. (Instructions and times may vary.)

Caramel Apple
Blondie Pie

The Ultimate Chocolate Pie

Tennessee Whiskey Pie

CARAMEL APPLE BLONDIE PIE

A store-bought piecrust can certainly make life easier. That said, this recipe doesn't fall short on a shortcut. Caramelized apples sit atop buttery, rich layers of cake underneath. I always put this dish together in my cast-iron skillet, baking it on the lower rack of the oven to turn out a perfectly flaky, crispy crust.

SERVES 8 TO 10 • HANDS-ON: 1 HOUR • TOTAL: 4 HOURS, 40 MINUTES, INCLUDING SAUCE

6 large Granny Smith apples (about 3 pounds)
1½ cups plus 2 tablespoons all-purpose flour
2 cups firmly packed light brown sugar
8 ounces (1 cup) salted butter
1½ teaspoons baking powder
½ teaspoon table salt
3 large eggs, lightly beaten
3 tablespoons bourbon
¾ cup coarsely chopped toasted pecans
½ (14.1-ounce) package refrigerated piecrusts
Apple Cider Caramel Sauce (recipe below)

1. Peel the apples, and cut into ¼-inch-thick wedges. Toss with 2 tablespoons flour and ½ cup of the brown sugar in a large bowl. Melt ¼ cup of the butter in a large skillet over medium-high; add the apple mixture, and sauté 15 minutes or until apples are tender and liquid is thickened. Remove from heat; cool completely (about 30 minutes).
2. Meanwhile, preheat the oven to 350°F. Melt remaining ¾ cup butter. Stir together 1½ cups flour, baking powder, and salt in a large bowl. Add the eggs, bourbon, ¾ cup melted butter, and remaining 1½ cups brown sugar, stirring until blended. Stir in the pecans.
3. Fit the piecrust into a 10-inch cast-iron skillet, gently pressing piecrust all the way up the sides of skillet. Spoon two-thirds of the apple mixture over bottom of piecrust, spreading and gently pressing apple slices into an even layer using the back of a spoon. Spoon the batter over the apple mixture; top with remaining apple mixture.
4. Place the pie on lower oven rack, and bake at 350°F for 1 hour and 10 minutes to 1 hour and 20 minutes or until a wooden pick inserted in center comes out with a few moist crumbs. Remove from oven; cool the pie completely on a wire rack.
5. Drizzle the cooled pie with ⅓ cup Apple Cider Caramel Sauce. Serve with remaining sauce.

APPLE CIDER CARAMEL SAUCE

1 cup (8 ounces) apple cider
1 cup firmly packed light brown sugar
4 ounces (½ cup) salted butter
¼ cup (2 ounces) whipping cream

Cook the cider in a 3-quart saucepan over medium, stirring often, 10 minutes or until reduced to ¼ cup. Stir in remaining ingredients. Bring to a boil over medium-high, stirring constantly; boil, stirring constantly, 2 minutes. Remove from heat, and cool completely. Refrigerate up to 1 week. To reheat, microwave at HIGH 10 to 15 seconds or just until warm; stir until smooth. Makes about 1¼ cups

THE ULTIMATE CHOCOLATE PIE

An old school staple, chocolate pie never goes out of style. What makes this the ultimate chocolate pie is the heavy dollops of chocolate whipped cream on top.

SERVES 10 • HANDS-ON: 1 HOUR, 20 MINUTES • TOTAL: 11 HOURS, INCLUDING WHIPPED CREAM

Crust
2 cups chocolate wafer cookie crumbs
½ cup finely chopped toasted pecans
¼ cup sugar
4 ounces (½ cup) salted butter, melted
Filling
¾ cup sugar
¼ cup cornstarch
¼ cup unsweetened cocoa
⅛ teaspoon table salt
2 cups (16 ounces) half-and-half
4 large egg yolks
1 (4-ounce) semisweet chocolate baking bar, finely chopped
½ (4-ounce) 60% cacao bittersweet chocolate baking bar, finely chopped
2 tablespoons salted butter
1 teaspoon vanilla extract
Mousse
¾ cup milk chocolate morsels
1 cup plus 3 tablespoons (about 11 ounces) heavy cream
Chocolate Whipped Cream (recipe below)
Garnish: chocolate wafer cookies

1. Make the Crust: Preheat the oven to 350°F. Lightly grease (with cooking spray) a 9-inch deep-dish pie plate. Pulse the first 3 ingredients in a food processor 4 or 5 times. Transfer the crumb mixture to a medium bowl; stir in ½ cup melted butter. Press on bottom, up sides, and onto rim of prepared pie plate. Bake at 350°F for 10 minutes. Cool on a wire rack.
2. Make the Filling: Whisk together ¾ cup sugar and next 3 ingredients in a large saucepan. Whisk together half-and-half and egg yolks in a bowl. Gradually whisk the egg mixture into sugar mixture. Cook over medium, whisking constantly, 6 to 8 minutes or just until the mixture begins to boil. Cook, whisking constantly, 1 more minute; remove from heat. Whisk in the semisweet chocolate and next 3 ingredients. Place plastic wrap directly on the warm filling. Let stand 30 minutes. Spread filling in cooled crust; place plastic wrap directly on filling, and chill 30 minutes.
3. Make the Mousse: Microwave the milk chocolate morsels and 3 tablespoons heavy cream in a medium bowl at MEDIUM (50% power) for 1 to 1½ minutes or until melted and smooth, stirring at 30-second intervals. Let stand 30 minutes, stirring occasionally. Beat 1 cup heavy cream at medium-high speed with an electric mixer until soft peaks form. Gently fold half of whipped cream into milk chocolate mixture until blended and smooth; fold in remaining whipped cream. Spread mousse over filling. Cover and chill 8 to 24 hours or until set. Top with the Chocolate Whipped Cream just before serving. Garnish, if desired.

CHOCOLATE WHIPPED CREAM

3 cups (24 ounces) heavy cream
2 tablespoons chocolate syrup
1 teaspoon vanilla extract
¼ cup sugar

Whisk together the cream and chocolate syrup in a bowl. Beat the cream mixture and vanilla at medium-high speed with an electric mixer until foamy; gradually add sugar, beating until soft peaks form. Makes about 6 cups

TENNESSEE WHISKEY PIE

I sometimes skip dessert, opting for a cocktail instead. Then I got smart—combining my love for booze and a sweet treat together to ensure I could enjoy the best of both worlds. Nothing about this pie is "light"—the combo of pecans and smoky-sweet bourbon produces a rich pie filling that is best enjoyed with another bourbon neat on the side. Go big, or go home.

SERVES 8 • HANDS-ON: 50 MINUTES
TOTAL: 3 HOURS, 30 MINUTES, INCLUDING WHIPPED CREAM AND SAUCE

Crust
½ tablespoon salted butter
¼ cup finely chopped pecans
Pinch of kosher salt
1¼ cups all-purpose flour
2 tablespoons granulated sugar
½ teaspoon table salt
2 ounces (¼ cup) cold salted butter, cubed
¼ cup cold shortening, cubed
3 to 4 tablespoons whole buttermilk

Filling
1 cup dark corn syrup
½ cup granulated sugar
½ cup firmly packed light brown sugar
¼ cup (2 ounces) Tennessee whiskey*
4 large eggs
2 ounces (¼ cup) salted butter, melted
2 teaspoons plain white cornmeal
2 teaspoons vanilla extract
½ teaspoon table salt
2½ cups lightly toasted pecan halves
Whiskey Whipped Cream (optional) (recipe opposite)
Easy Caramel Sauce (optional) (recipe opposite)

1. Make the Crust: Melt ½ tablespoon butter in a small skillet over medium, swirling to coat sides of pan. Add ¼ cup finely chopped pecans, and sauté 2 minutes or until fragrant and lightly toasted. Sprinkle the pecan mixture with a pinch of salt. Remove the pecans from skillet, and cool completely. Reserve for use in Step 4.

2. Pulse the flour and next 2 ingredients in a food processor 3 or 4 times or until well combined. Add the cubed cold butter and the cold shortening; pulse until the mixture is crumbly. Drizzle 3 tablespoons buttermilk over the flour mixture, and pulse just until moist clumps form. (Add up to 1 tablespoon buttermilk, 1 teaspoon at a time, if necessary.) Shape the dough into a flat disk, and wrap tightly with plastic wrap. Chill the dough at least 1 hour.

3. Meanwhile, make the Filling: Place the corn syrup and next 3 ingredients in a large saucepan, and bring to a boil over medium, whisking constantly. Cook, whisking constantly, 2 minutes; remove from heat. Whisk together the eggs and next 4 ingredients in a bowl. Gradually whisk about one-fourth of the hot corn syrup mixture into the egg mixture; gradually add the egg mixture to remaining hot corn syrup mixture, whisking constantly. Stir in 2½ cups lightly toasted pecan halves; cool completely (about 30 minutes).

4. Preheat the oven to 325°F. Lightly grease (with cooking spray) a 9-inch pie plate. Unwrap the dough, and roll into a 13-inch circle on a lightly floured surface. Sprinkle the dough with the sautéed pecans (reserved from Step 1). Place a piece of plastic wrap over the dough and the pecans, and lightly roll the pecans into the dough. Fit the dough into prepared pie plate.

Fold edges under, and crimp. Pour the cooled filling into the prepared crust.
5. Bake at 325°F for 50 to 55 minutes or until set; cool the pie completely on a wire rack (about 2 hours) before slicing. Serve with the Whiskey Whipped Cream and Easy Caramel Sauce, if desired.

*Water or apple juice may be substituted.

WHISKEY WHIPPED CREAM

1 cup (8 ounces) heavy cream
1 teaspoon Tennessee whiskey
3 tablespoons powdered sugar

Beat the cream and the whiskey at medium-high speed with an electric mixer until foamy. Gradually add the powdered sugar, beating until soft peaks form. Makes about 1½ cups

EASY CARAMEL SAUCE

1 cup sugar
⅓ cup (about 3 ounces) water
2 teaspoons fresh lemon juice
1 cup (8 ounces) heavy cream
2 teaspoons vanilla extract
Pinch of sea salt

1. Bring the sugar, water, and lemon juice (to prevent crystals from forming) to a boil in a tall, heavy saucepan over medium-high; boil 3 minutes or until sugar melts and liquid is clear, swirling pan occasionally. Cover; boil 1 minute.
2. Remove lid. Boil, gently swirling often and checking color and temperature every 5 to 10 seconds, about 4 minutes or until a candy thermometer reaches 345° to 350°F and mixture is medium to dark amber in color. Remove from heat.
3. Gradually whisk in cream. (Mixture will bubble and spatter.) Cook, whisking constantly, over low 1 minute or until smooth. Remove from heat; stir in vanilla and sea salt. Transfer to a serving bowl or pitcher. Chill, covered, up to 1 week. Makes about 2 cups

STRAWBERRY-LEMON-BUTTERMILK ICEBOX PIE *with* GINGERSNAP CRUST

This recipe might have a long name, but as soon as your fork cuts into this chilled pie, your taste buds will echo a chorus of gratitude.

SERVES 8 • HANDS-ON: 40 MINUTES • TOTAL: 6 HOURS, 40 MINUTES, INCLUDING CRUST

1 (14-ounce) can sweetened condensed milk
1 tablespoon loosely packed lemon zest
½ cup (4 ounces) fresh lemon juice (about 4 lemons)
½ cup plus 3 tablespoons strawberry jam
3 large egg yolks
¼ cup (2 ounces) whole buttermilk
Gingersnap Crust, baked (recipe below)
1 pound sliced strawberries

1. Preheat the oven to 325°F. Whisk together the sweetened condensed milk, lemon zest, lemon juice, and ½ cup strawberry jam in a medium bowl.
2. Beat the egg yolks with a handheld mixer in a medium bowl at high speed 4 to 5 minutes or until yolks become pale and ribbons form on surface of mixture when beater is lifted. Gradually whisk in the sweetened condensed milk mixture, and whisk until thoroughly combined; whisk in the buttermilk. Pour the mixture into the prepared crust.
3. Bake at 325°F for 20 to 25 minutes or until set around edges. (Pie will be slightly jiggly.) Cool on a wire rack 1 hour. Cover the pie with lightly greased (with cooking spray) plastic wrap, and freeze 4 to 6 hours.
4. Microwave remaining 3 tablespoons strawberry jam in a medium-size microwave-safe bowl at HIGH 20 seconds. Stir the sliced strawberries into jam. Top the pie with the strawberry mixture just before serving.

GINGERSNAP CRUST

1½ cups crushed gingersnaps
¼ cup sugar
1 teaspoon kosher salt
3 ounces (6 tablespoons) salted butter, melted

Lightly grease (with cooking spray) a 9-inch regular pie plate or 9-inch deep-dish pie plate. Process the crushed cookies, sugar, and salt in a food processor until finely crushed and well combined. Add the melted butter, and process until thoroughly combined. Press on bottom, up sides, and onto lip of prepared pie plate. Freeze 30 minutes to 1 hour or while preparing filling.
Makes 1 (9-inch) regular piecrust or 1 (9-inch) deep-dish piecrust

Note: For baked piecrusts, preheat oven to 325°F. Bake the crust at 325°F for 8 to 10 minutes or until lightly browned.

Grilled Banana Splits

PB&B Pudding

GRILLED BANANA SPLITS

A grilled piece of fruit is one of my favorite go-to desserts. The high heat from the grill allows the natural sugars in the fruit to caramelize, while also lending a smoky essence.

SERVES 6 • HANDS-ON: 15 MINUTES • TOTAL: 30 MINUTES

¼ cup chopped pecans
¼ cup sweetened flaked coconut
6 unpeeled small bananas with green tips
Vegetable cooking spray
6 fresh or canned pineapple slices
1 pint vanilla ice cream
1 pint chocolate frozen yogurt
Chocolate sauce
Garnish: maraschino cherries

1. Coat cold cooking grate of grill with cooking spray. Preheat the grill to 300° to 350°F (medium).
2. Preheat the oven to 350°F. Place the pecans in a single layer in a shallow pan. Place the coconut in a single layer in another shallow pan. Bake the pecans and the coconut at 350°F for 7 to 8 minutes or until toasted and pecans are fragrant, stirring occasionally.
3. Peel the bananas, and cut in half lengthwise. Coat the bananas with cooking spray. Grill the pineapple slices, covered with grill lid, 4 minutes on each side or until lightly caramelized. Grill the banana halves 1 to 2 minutes on each side or until lightly caramelized.
4. Chop the grilled pineapple. Arrange 2 grilled banana halves in each of 6 (8-ounce) banana-split dishes or other serving bowls. Scoop ¼ cup of the vanilla ice cream and ¼ cup of the chocolate frozen yogurt into each dish between the banana slices. Top each with 1 tablespoon of the chocolate sauce, 1 chopped pineapple slice, 2 teaspoons pecans, and 2 teaspoons coconut. Serve immediately. Garnish with maraschino cherries.

PB&B PUDDING

This is an excellent picnic dish—I like to layer the pudding in half-pint jars with room for garnish.

SERVES 10 • HANDS-ON: 30 MINUTES • TOTAL: 2 HOURS, 30 MINUTES

3 cups (24 ounces) milk
4 large egg yolks
1 cup sugar
⅓ cup all-purpose flour
⅛ teaspoon table salt
½ cup creamy peanut butter
2 small ripe bananas, diced
2 teaspoons vanilla extract
1 cup chopped roasted, salted peanuts
1 cup coarsely crushed vanilla wafers
Garnishes: frozen whipped topping, thawed; cooked, crumbled bacon

1. Cook the first 5 ingredients in a large saucepan over medium-low, whisking constantly, 15 to 20 minutes or until thickened. Remove from heat; whisk in the peanut butter until blended. Stir in the diced bananas and the vanilla.
2. Combine peanuts and vanilla wafers. Divide 1 cup of the peanut mixture among 10 (8-ounce) jars. Top with pudding and remaining peanut mixture. Cover and chill 2 to 24 hours. Garnish, if desired.

FLOURLESS PEANUT BUTTER-CHOCOLATE CHIP COOKIES

I've gotta tell y'all, this is one good cookie! And I have even better news—this cookie also happens to be entirely gluten-free! Hold on a second, I didn't say flavor-free. The peanut butter and chocolate combine to produce a dense, moist cookie that's both feel good and delicious.

MAKES 2 DOZEN • HANDS-ON: 15 MINUTES • TOTAL: 1 HOUR, 15 MINUTES

Parchment paper
1 cup creamy peanut butter
¾ cup sugar
1 large egg
½ teaspoon baking soda
¼ teaspoon table salt
1 cup semisweet chocolate morsels

1. Preheat the oven to 350°F. Line baking sheets with parchment paper. Stir together the peanut butter and next 4 ingredients in a medium bowl until well blended. Stir in the chocolate morsels.
2. Drop the dough by rounded tablespoonfuls 2 inches apart onto prepared baking sheets.
3. Bake at 350°F for 12 to 14 minutes or until puffed and lightly browned. Cool on baking sheets on a wire rack 5 minutes. Transfer to wire rack, and cool 15 minutes.

CONDIMENTS

CHUNKY HOT SAUCE

In my home, hot sauce is always a welcomed condiment on the table. Rest assured, I take no offense if you want to shake on a few shots of sauce to amplify your meal. The key to making this sauce is all about practicing a bit of patience—fermentation is the secret. From there, you can chose your own blend of chiles, and either puree the sauce in a chunky form, or press it through a wire-mesh strainer to produce a looser, smoother consistency.

MAKES 4 CUPS • HANDS-ON: 15 MINUTES • TOTAL: 15 MINUTES, PLUS 1 WEEK STAND TIME

1 pound fresh hot chiles (such as Fresno), washed and stemmed
2½ tablespoons kosher salt
Cheesecloth
2 cups (16 ounces) white vinegar

1. Process the chiles and the salt in a food processor about 30 seconds or until minced, stopping to scrape down sides as needed. Transfer the chile mixture to a sterilized 1-quart glass jar. Cover with cheesecloth, and let stand in a cool, dry place 2 days.
2. Remove cheesecloth, and stir in the vinegar. Cover the mixture with cheesecloth, and let stand in a cool, dry place 5 days. (Skim and discard any film from surface, if necessary.) Cover jar with a tight-fitting lid; refrigerate up to 6 months.

CANDIED JALAPEÑOS

Make no mistake, the heat from a fresh jalapeño chile can either be super tolerable, or knock you on your back! For that very reason, I've chosen to take the more mild, pickled jalapeño and create a fiery-sweet recipe that's a great condiment on a pork sandwich or BBQ nachos—heck, even on a cracker with sharp Cheddar cheese. It is best to allow these guys to chill for at least two days to take on as much flavor as possible.

MAKES 1⅓ CUPS • HANDS-ON: 10 MINUTES • TOTAL: 10 MINUTES, PLUS 48 HOURS STAND TIME

1 (12-ounce) jar pickled jalapeño chile slices
4 red chile peppers, sliced
¾ cup sugar
1 teaspoon loosely packed lime zest

Drain the pickled jalapeño chile slices, discarding the liquid and reserving jar and lid. Toss together the jalapeño slices, red chile pepper slices, sugar, and lime zest. Let stand 5 minutes, stirring occasionally. Spoon into reserved jar, scraping any remaining sugar mixture from bowl into jar. Cover with lid, and chill 48 hours to 1 week, shaking jar several times a day to dissolve any sugar that settles.

Blue
Cheese
Ranch
Lemony Ranch
Avocado
Ranch

HERBED BUTTERMILK RANCH DRESSING

Fresh herbs, garlic, and buttermilk all combine to take a traditional Ranch dressing to the next level. For fun, I've laid out several varieties to the base recipe—I highly encourage you to take each one on a test drive.

MAKES ABOUT 1½ CUPS • HANDS-ON: 10 MINUTES
TOTAL: 40 MINUTES, INCLUDING 30 MINUTES CHILLING TIME

1 cup (8 ounces) whole buttermilk
¼ cup mayonnaise
¼ cup sour cream
1 small garlic clove, pressed
2 tablespoons minced shallot
1 tablespoon finely chopped fresh flat-leaf parsley
2 teaspoons finely chopped fresh chives
1 teaspoon kosher salt
1 teaspoon coarse-grain Dijon mustard
½ teaspoon freshly ground black pepper
¼ teaspoon hot sauce

Combine all the ingredients in a 1-quart glass jar with a tight-fitting lid. Cover and shake vigorously to blend. Chill 30 minutes. Refrigerate in covered jar up to 1 week. Shake well before serving.

Lemony Ranch: Make the Herbed Buttermilk Ranch Dressing as directed, adding ¼ cup fresh lemon juice, 3 tablespoons extra virgin olive oil, and 2 teaspoons honey to jar before shaking. Makes about 2 cups

Blue Cheese Ranch: Make the Herbed Buttermilk Ranch Dressing as directed, adding 2 ounces mashed blue cheese, 2 ounces crumbled blue cheese, 2 teaspoons chopped fresh chives, ½ teaspoon freshly ground black pepper, and ½ teaspoon paprika to jar before shaking. Makes about 2 cups

Avocado Ranch: Make the Herbed Buttermilk Ranch Dressing as directed, adding 1 ripe mashed avocado, 2 tablespoons minced jalapeño chile, 2 tablespoons hot sauce, 4 teaspoons fresh lime juice, and ½ teaspoon kosher salt to jar before shaking. Makes about 2½ cups

PICKLED OKRA

For any true Southerner, a jar or two of pickled okra in the cupboard is as essential as having sweet tea in the fridge.

MAKES 7 (1-PINT) JARS • HANDS-ON: 40 MINUTES • TOTAL: 12 HOURS, 40 MINUTES

1 (9-piece) canning kit, including canner, jar lifter, and canning rack
7 (1-pint) canning jars
2½ pounds small fresh okra
7 small fresh green chiles
7 garlic cloves
2 tablespoons plus 1 teaspoon dill seeds
4 cups (32 ounces) white vinegar
½ cup table salt
¼ cup sugar
4 cups (32 ounces) water

1. Bring canner half-full with water to a boil; simmer. Meanwhile, place jars in a large stockpot with water to cover; bring to a boil, and simmer. Place bands and lids in a large saucepan with water to cover; bring to a boil, and simmer. Remove hot jars 1 at a time using jar lifter.
2. Pack the okra into hot jars, filling to ½ inch from top. Place 1 chile, 1 garlic clove, and 1 teaspoon dill seeds in each jar. Bring the vinegar, salt, sugar, and 4 cups water to a boil over medium-high. Pour over the okra, filling to ½ inch from top.
3. Wipe jar rims; cover at once with metal lids, and screw on bands (snug but not too tight). Place jars in canning rack, and place in simmering water in canner. Add additional boiling water as needed to cover by 1 to 2 inches.
4. Bring water to a rolling boil; boil 10 minutes. Remove from heat. Cool jars in canner 5 minutes. Transfer jars to a cutting board; cool 12 to 24 hours. Test seals of jars by pressing center of each lid. If lids do not pop, jars are properly sealed. Store in a cool, dry place at room temperature up to 1 year.

PICKLED OKRA SALSA

I like serving this salsa conventionally with blue corn chips, as part of a cheese platter, or as a topping on proteins such as grilled chicken, pork, or fish.

MAKES ABOUT 1½ CUPS • HANDS-ON: 10 MINUTES • TOTAL: 10 MINUTES

5 whole pickled okra, sliced
½ cup chopped sweet onion
4 teaspoons chopped fresh cilantro
1 teaspoon fresh lime juice
¼ teaspoon table salt
⅛ teaspoon freshly ground black pepper
1 (14.5-ounce) can diced tomatoes with mild green chiles, drained

Pulse the first 6 ingredients and half of the tomatoes in a food processor 4 to 6 times or until thoroughly combined. Stir in remaining diced tomatoes. Serve immediately, or cover and chill. Store in refrigerator up to 7 days. If refrigerated, let stand at room temperature 15 minutes before serving.

Ball

SOUTHERN GIARDINIERA

I'm a dill pickle guy, but I've got to tell y'all, this bread-and-butter-style brine works super well with the mess of pickled veggies in this recipe. Red pearl onions can sometimes be hard to source—though they do add a nice bit of color to the mix. If you can't find them, sub Vidalia or yellow sweet onions instead.

SERVES 12 TO 14 • HANDS-ON: 30 MINUTES
TOTAL: 1 HOUR, 30 MINUTES, PLUS 1 DAY STAND TIME

1 pound multicolored baby carrots with tops
4 cups (32 ounces) apple cider vinegar
1½ cups granulated sugar
1 cup firmly packed light brown sugar
½ cup kosher salt
⅓ cup molasses
1½ tablespoons yellow mustard seeds
1 tablespoon whole black peppercorns
1 (10-ounce) package fresh red pearl onions, peeled and halved
2 cups small fresh broccoli florets
2 jalapeño chiles, sliced
1 (8-ounce) package sweet mini peppers
1 medium fennel bulb, sliced

1. Trim tops from the carrots, leaving 1 inch of greenery on each; peel the carrots. Cut the carrots in half lengthwise. Bring the vinegar, granulated sugar, brown sugar, salt, molasses, mustard seeds, and peppercorns to a boil in a medium-size nonaluminum saucepan over medium-high, stirring until sugars and salt dissolve. Reduce heat to medium; add the carrots and the onions, and simmer 3 minutes, stirring occasionally.
2. Place the broccoli and next 3 ingredients in a large heatproof bowl; pour the hot vinegar mixture over the vegetables. Cool completely (about 1 hour). Stir occasionally while mixture cools.
3. Transfer the vegetables to 2 hot sterilized 1-quart jars, using a slotted spoon and filling to 1 inch from top. Pour the cooled vinegar mixture from bowl into a liquid measuring cup with a pour spout. Pour enough vinegar mixture into jars to cover the vegetables, and discard remaining vinegar mixture. Cover with metal lids, and screw on bands. Let stand 24 hours before using. Refrigerate in an airtight container up to 2 weeks.

Crunchy Summer Salsa

Sweet Corn
Relish
Green Tomato
Relish
Chowchow

CRUNCHY SUMMER SALSA

It's the cucumber, my friends, that adds a nice earthy flavor and addictive crunch to this fresh salsa. For a twist, I'll go along with this recipe, only chopping the peaches and cucumbers into larger portions and topping the whole mixture with crumbled feta to create a fresh salad to serve as a side.

MAKES ABOUT 1¾ CUPS • HANDS-ON: 10 MINUTES • TOTAL: 10 MINUTES

1 cup diced fresh peaches
½ cup diced cucumber
1 jalapeño chile, seeded (if desired) and diced
1 garlic clove, minced
3 tablespoons chopped fresh cilantro
2 tablespoons fresh lime juice
½ teaspoon kosher salt

Stir together the peaches, cucumber, jalapeño chile, minced garlic, cilantro, lime juice, and salt in a small bowl.

GREEN TOMATO RELISH

Pucker up, buttercup. Tangy, sour green tomatoes are subbed for pickles to create a unique relish that's perfect when served on grilled hotdogs or a smoked bologna sandwich.

MAKES ABOUT 4 CUPS • HANDS-ON: 40 MINUTES • TOTAL: 2 HOURS, 10 MINUTES

1½ pounds green tomatoes, quartered
1 red bell pepper
1 poblano pepper
1 large white onion, sliced
1 cup matchstick carrots
½ cup (4 ounces) water
2 cups (16 ounces) white vinegar
1 cup sugar
1 tablespoon kosher salt
1 tablespoon mustard seeds
¼ teaspoon ground turmeric
⅛ teaspoon ground cloves
⅛ teaspoon ground allspice

1. Remove and discard the seeds and the ribs from the tomatoes and the peppers. Cut into thin slices.
2. Bring the onion, carrots, tomatoes, peppers, ½ cup water, and 1 cup of the vinegar to a boil in a large stockpot over high; reduce heat to medium-low, and simmer, stirring occasionally, 30 minutes. Drain.
3. Return the vegetables to stockpot, and stir in the sugar, next 5 ingredients, and remaining 1 cup vinegar. Bring to a boil over medium-high; reduce heat to medium-low, and simmer 5 minutes. Cool completely. Transfer to a jar; screw on lid, and chill 30 minutes. Store in refrigerator up to 1 week.

SWEET CORN RELISH

Stop cooking your corn and "pickle" it instead. Sliced off the cob, fresh corn kernels meet a vinegary mixture that actually cooks and softens the corn. The horseradish provides a sweet-heat kick that makes this relish a versatile topping for hearty grilled veggies such as zucchini, eggplant, or squash, and proteins including grilled pork, fish, or chicken.

MAKES ABOUT 3 CUPS • HANDS-ON: 20 MINUTES • TOTAL: 45 MINUTES

1 cup (8 ounces) apple cider vinegar
¼ cup sugar
1 teaspoon kosher salt
1 teaspoon prepared horseradish
2 cups fresh corn kernels (about 4 ears)
2 medium zucchini, diced
½ cup diced plum tomato
½ cup thinly sliced scallions
1 tablespoon chopped fresh flat-leaf parsley

1. Stir together the vinegar, sugar, and salt in a small saucepan. Bring to a boil over medium-high; reduce heat to medium, and simmer 10 minutes or until reduced to about ½ cup. Remove from heat, and let stand 15 minutes. Stir in the horseradish.
2. Stir together the corn and next 4 ingredients in a medium bowl. Add the vinegar mixture, and toss to coat. Serve immediately, or cover and chill up to 3 days.

CHOWCHOW

This is a "catchall" condiment featuring crunchy cabbage and nearly anything else you can pull out of the fridge. Chowchow is as married to a pork sandwich as fresh peaches were meant for homemade ice cream. Add in some fresh sliced jalapeño slices for extra heat.

MAKES ABOUT 3 CUPS • HANDS-ON: 25 MINUTES • TOTAL: 4 HOURS, 5 MINUTES

3 cups chopped cabbage
¾ cup chopped onion
¾ cup chopped green tomatoes
½ cup chopped green bell pepper
½ cup chopped red bell pepper
1 tablespoon pickling salt
¾ cup sugar
½ cup white vinegar
¼ cup (2 ounces) water
¾ teaspoon mustard seeds
¼ teaspoon celery seeds
¼ teaspoon ground turmeric
½ teaspoon red pepper flakes (optional)
1 jalapeño chile, seeded and finely chopped (optional)

Stir together the cabbage, onion, green tomatoes, chopped green and red bell peppers, and pickling salt. Cover and chill 2 to 8 hours. Transfer the mixture to a Dutch oven. Stir in the sugar, vinegar, ¼ cup water, mustard seeds, celery seeds, turmeric, and, if desired, red pepper flakes. Bring to a boil over medium-high; reduce heat to medium, and simmer 3 minutes. Cool to room temperature (about 30 minutes). Stir in the jalapeño, if desired. Cover and chill 1 to 8 hours before serving.

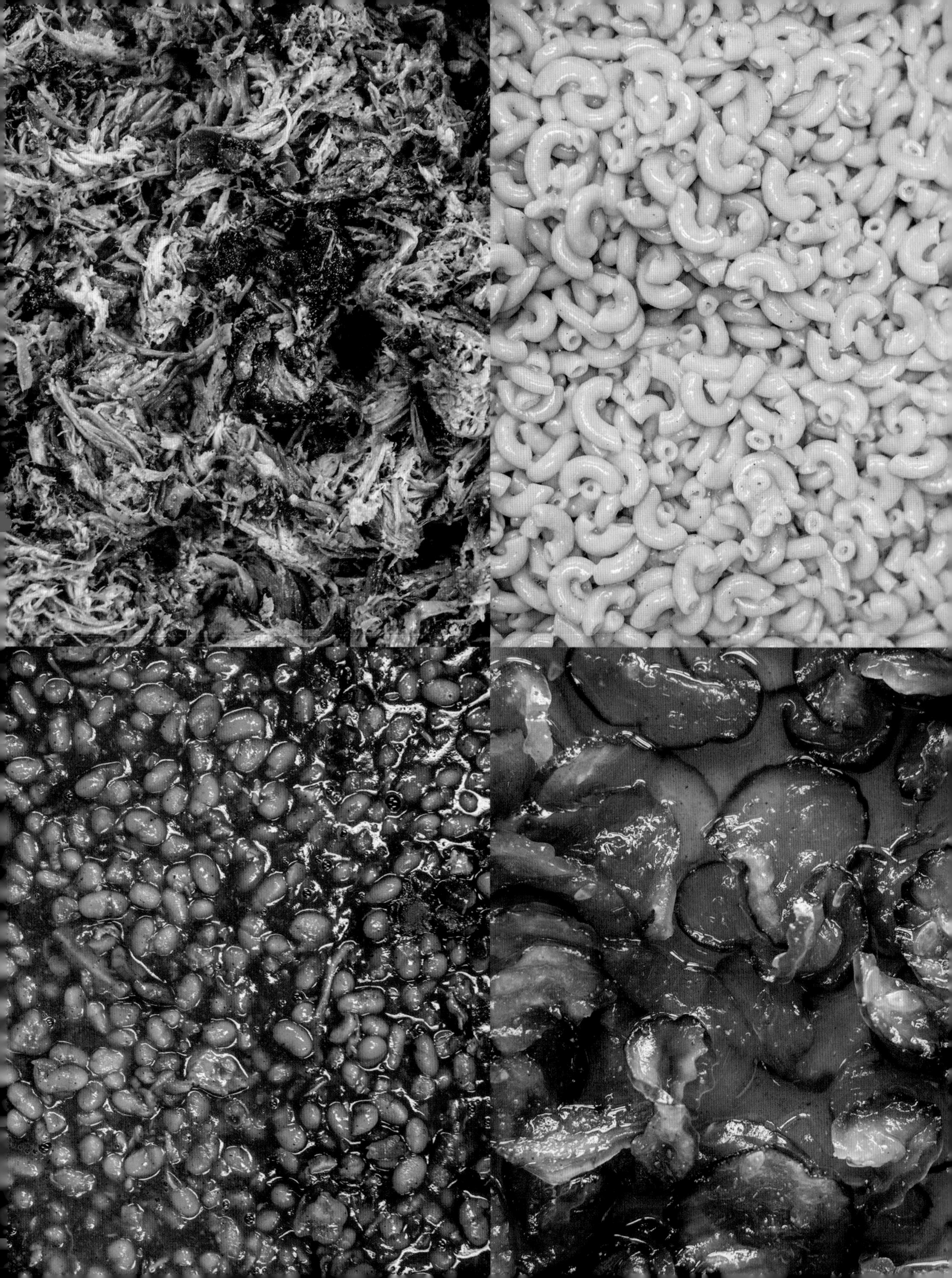

ACKNOWLEDGMENTS

I would like to thank the pitmasters, those kind men and women featured in this book who shared their passion, talents, recipes, and stories with me. And also to all of those not featured in this book—professionals, amateurs, and weekend warriors. American BBQ is a grand tradition worth honoring, savoring, and preserving—carry on.

To my agent, Stacey Glick, thank you for the endless support and guidance, as well as your friendship. To my editor, Katherine Cobbs—we did it! What an adventure this book was—thank you for providing me with the opportunity to be a part of creating this beautiful book.

Photographer Andrea Behrends—thank you for jumping into my world of crazy schedules, putting up with my strange stories while on the road, and, of course, trusting your life to me when flying in the plane. Your work speaks for itself—a true documentation of some of the most beautiful people and places I'd ever hoped to document—thank you for bringing it all to life.

To the team at *Southern Living,* Oxmoor House, and Time Inc. Books—it takes an army. I would like to thank all of those who played a part in creating this book, as well as supporting me throughout the years. I'd like to specifically say thanks to Sid Evans, Margot Schupf, Allison Devlin, Anja Schmidt, Bryan Christian, Robbie Melvin, and Hunter Lewis.

Last but not least, to my beautiful wife, Callie, and my loving daughter, Vivienne . . . and to our next baby on the way. I would not be able to do any of this without your love, support, and day-to-day sacrifice. Thank you—I love you.

METRIC EQUIVALENTS

The information in the following charts is provided to help cooks outside the United States successfully use the recipes in this book. All equivalents are approximate.

EQUIVALENTS FOR DIFFERENT TYPES OF INGREDIENTS

Standard Cup	Fine Powder (ex. flour)	Grain (ex. rice)	Granular (ex. sugar)	Liquid Solids (ex. butter)	Liquid (ex. milk)
1	140 g	150 g	190 g	200 g	240 ml
¾	105 g	113 g	143 g	150 g	180 ml
⅔	93 g	100 g	125 g	133 g	160 ml
½	70 g	75 g	95 g	100 g	120 ml
⅓	47 g	50 g	63 g	67 g	80 ml
¼	35 g	38 g	48 g	50 g	60 ml
⅛	18 g	19 g	24 g	25 g	30 ml

LIQUID INGREDIENTS BY VOLUME

¼ tsp =			1 ml	
½ tsp =			2 ml	
1 tsp =			5 ml	
3 tsp = 1 Tbsp =		½ fl oz =	15 ml	
2 Tbsp =	⅛ cup =	1 fl oz =	30 ml	
4 Tbsp =	¼ cup =	2 fl oz =	60 ml	
5⅓ Tbsp =	⅓ cup =	3 fl oz =	80 ml	
8 Tbsp =	½ cup =	4 fl oz =	120 ml	
10⅔ Tbsp =	⅔ cup =	5 fl oz =	160 ml	
12 Tbsp =	¾ cup =	6 fl oz =	180 ml	
16 Tbsp =	1 cup =	8 fl oz =	240 ml	
1 pt =	2 cups =	16 fl oz =	480 ml	
1 qt =	4 cups =	32 fl oz =	960 ml	
		33 fl oz =	1000 ml =	1 l

DRY INGREDIENTS BY WEIGHT

(To convert ounces to grams, multiply the number of ounces by 30.)

1 oz	=	1/16 lb	=	30 g
4 oz	=	¼ lb	=	120 g
8 oz	=	½ lb	=	240 g
12 oz	=	¾ lb	=	360 g
16 oz	=	1 lb	=	480 g

LENGTH

(To convert inches to centimeters, multiply the number of inches by 2.5.)

1 in =			2.5 cm	
6 in =	½ ft	=	15 cm	
12 in =	1 ft	=	30 cm	
36 in =	3 ft =	1 yd =	90 cm	
40 in =			100 cm =	1 m

COOKING/OVEN TEMPERATURES

	Fahrenheit	Celsius	Gas Mark
Freeze Water	32° F	0° C	
Room Temperature	68° F	20° C	
Boil Water	212° F	100° C	
Bake	325° F	160° C	3
	350° F	180° C	4
	375° F	190° C	5
	400° F	200° C	6
	425° F	220° C	7
	450° F	230° C	8
Broil			Grill

A

Alabama, 29, 37, 38
Arkansas, 29, 125
Arkansas State University, 64
Arkansas-style barbecue, 125
The Art Institute of Atlanta, 84
Atlanta, 27, 83
Auburn University, 27
Austin, 135

B

barbacoa, 13
barbe à queue, 13
BAR-BEER-CUE-PIG, 19th century advertisements, 14
BBQ Belt, 12, 22, 29
B-Daddy's BBQ, Helotes, Texas, 132–145
  Allbritton, Justin, 133
  all-natural, hormone-free beef, 143
  Anderson, B.A. (Bernard Allen), 133
    USA BMX, 133
  Anderson, B.R. (Bernard Ray), 133–137, 138, 141, 143
    "BBQ saved my life," 134, 137
    food truck, 134, 135, 138
    University of Texas at San Antonio, 133
  Anderson, Haley, 135
  Anderson, Kyle, 135, 141
    "spending time with Dad," 135
  brisket, 135
  FBI, 133, 135
  Pennington, Todd, 134
  pork butt. . .drenched in Dr Pepper, 135, 138
    "pulled" with the help of an electric drill, 135
  RO-Man Pork Puller, 138
Big Butts BBQ, Leachville, Arkansas, 124–131
  "Arkansas redneck" smoker, 126
  authentic Southern hospitality, 126
  charcoal smoking, 125, 126, 128
  dedication to their family and the community, 126
  focus on pork, 125
  group of retirees
    Eleanor, 126
    Ms. Motely, 126
    Pauly & Leon, 126
    Rita, 126
  Robertson, Forrest, 125, 126, 128
    caterer at-large and day-to-day pitmaster, 126
  Robertson, Marti, 125, 126
  Robertson, O.L., 125
  Robertson, Rodney, 125–127
  Robertson, ShaeLyn, 126
  rotisserie-style smoker, 128
Birmingham, 38
Bloomington, Indiana, 50
Bogart's Smoke House, St. Louis, Missouri, 62–71
  Steele, Skip, 63–65, 69
    Arkansas State University, 64
    executive chef, 64
    hybrid form of barbecue, 64
    Marine Surveyor, 64
    Memphis, 63
    shipman's journal, 69
    "test kitchen," 64, 65
  Time + Temperature = Results, 63
boudin, 49, 50, 51
Brownsville, Tennessee, 107, 108
Burn Co. Barbecue, Tulsa, Oklahoma, 72–81
  Corcoran, Nick, 73, 75
  Derner, Richard, 75
    The Hideaway restaurant, 75
  fire-based methods, 75, 77
  Hasty-Bake grills, 73, 74, 75, 77
  Kus, Craig, 81
  Myers, Adam, 73–75, 77, 78
    Oklahoma BBQ is a bit of a "'tweener" style, 75, 76
    Oklahoma State University, 74
  smoked bologna, aka Oklahoma tenderloin, 73
  "a whole bunch of things" for servicemen, 73
Butts To Go, Pell City, Alabama, 36–47
  consistency, 39
  Gadsden, Alabama, 37
  Hardin, Mary, 38
  Jackson, Tim, 38
  low-and-slow method, 45
  Reich, David, 37
    Printup Hotel, 37
  Reich, Robert D., 37
    Reich Hotel, 37
  Reich, Wade, 37–41, 42, 45
    "An inconsistent restaurant will shutter prior to one that serves bad food consistently." 39, 41
    "Poppos," 37
    "Texas crutch" method, 42
  Rooms To Go, 37, 39
  Sevin, Emile, chef, 37
  Texaco service station, 37, 38
  Wallace, Dan, 38

C

charcoal, 23, 24, 125, 126
  briquettes, 23, 128
  chimney or electric starter, 23
  and creating a "reverse volcano," 23, 24
  and lighter fluid, 23
  lighting all the charcoal at one time, classic method, 23
  lump, 23, 75
  Minion method of lighting, 23
"chipped," 120, 122
chipped mutton, 118
Closed Pit, 22
cookout, 13
The Country's Quilt of 'Que, 29

D

Daegu, South Korea, 84
Dallas, 135
direct heat, 19, 21
dry rub, 29

E

Eastern Carolina, 70, 147, 153
East Texas, 84
Eunice, Louisiana, 49

F

Firebud Brands, 27
Florence, South Carolina, 161
food truck, 118, 134, 135, 138
French gastronomy, 27

G

Gadsden, Alabama, 37
Printup Hotel, 37
Reich Hotel, 37
Reich, Wade, 37
Gas, Charcoal, Egg, Barrel, and Commercial Smokers, 22
Georgia, 29, 33
Goldsboro, North Carolina, 147
greatest generation, 149
Griffin, Lloyd, Griffin's Barbecue, 147

H

Hastings, Grant, founder of Hasty-Bake grills, 74, 75
show-and-tell sales technique, 74
Hasty-Bake grills, 73, 74, 75, 77
Heirloom Market BBQ, Atlanta, Georgia, 82–93
Lee, Jiyeon, 83–85, 90, 93
Daegu, South Korea, 84
Korean pop star, 83
Le Cordon Bleu in Atlanta, 83
"the most famous Korean in Georgia. . .Look her up," 83, 89
Taylor, Cody, 83–85, 87, 93
The Art Institute of Atlanta, 84
East Texas, 84
Knoxville, 84
wood for heat and smoke, 84, 87
Helen's BBQ, Brownsville, Tennessee, 106–115
formerly known as Curly & Lynn's, 108
hickory and oak smoke, 111
smoked bologna sandwich, 107
Turner, Helen, 106–109, 111, 115
cook by feel and a whole lot of love, 107
"I just do," 107, 109
Turner, Reginald, 109
Haywood Company factory, 109
Helotes, Texas, 133
hickory, 25, 28, 73, 75, 84, 87, 108, 111, 118
Highway 281, 134
Houston, 134, 135
The Hybrid Method, 24
gas-assist cookers, 24

I

I-20, 37
indirect heat, 14, 19, 21, 22, 128

J

Johnson, Lady Bird, 119
Johnson's Boucanière, Lafayette, Louisiana, 48–61
closed pit, custom-built, 50
"Hot Boudin To-Day!," 49, 51
Johnson, Arneastor, 49
Johnson's Grocery, Eunice, Louisiana, 49
Johnson, Wallace, 49
"to-day it's, you know, sort of like my signature," 52
live oak, 50
"plate lunch," 50
Rauls, Stevie, 55
Walls, Greg, 49–51, 55, 56, 61
Bloomington, Indiana, 50
custom smokers, 55
Walls, Lori Johnson, 49–51, 55, 56, 61
Jonesboro, Arkansas, 64

K

Kansas, 75
Kansas City, 29
Kenly, North Carolina, 147
Kentucky, 29, 32
mutton, 29, 32
kettle smokers, 23
Knoxville, 84
komodo-style (egg) smokers, 22, 23

L

Lafayette, Louisiana, 49, 50, 51
Las Vegas, 64
Latta, South Carolina, 161
Leachville, Arkansas, 125
Le Cordon Bleu in Atlanta, 83
Liquid Smoke, 28
Lockhart, 135
London, 38
Louisiana, 29
low and slow, 45, 87, 108, 162, 165

M

Manhattan, 64
McCord, Michael, 27, 28
Firebud Brands, 27
signature "Slap Sauce," 27
three unwritten commandments of barbecue sauce, 28
meat and three, 50, 84
Memphis, 29, 63, 108
Meridian, Mississippi, 95
North Hills neighborhood, 95
mesquite, 25, 28
Mild Smoke: alder, maple, peach, plum, apple, cherry, 25
Mississippi, 29, 69
Missouri, 29, 125
Montreal, 64
Morganfield, 117
Music City, 39
mutton, 32, 118, 120
finely chopped by hand, aka "chipped," 120

N

Nashville, 50
New York, 64
North Alabama, 29, 32
North Carolina, 29, 30, 147, 153, 161

O

oak, 25, 28, 50, 84, 87, 108, 111, 147
Oklahoma, 29
Oklahoma State University, 74, 75
Open Pit, 21
oxygen, 24

P

paprika, 45
Paris, 38
Peak Brothers Bar-B-Que, Waverly, Kentucky, 116–123
the Coon Supper, 118
Greenwell, Grover, 117
hickory coals, 118
McKamey, Jerry, 117
mutton, 118, 120
open pit, 118
Peak, Barker, 117
Peak, Buddy, 117, 118
food truck, 118
Irene, Debbie, Eddie, Tony, Bobby, and Billy Steve, 117
persistence, 117, 119
Rich, Irene, 116–119, 122
"We don't call it sauce, honey, it's just called dip," 121
Pee Dee Native American tribe, 161
Pee Dee River, 161
Philippines, 95
pig, 13, 14
Piggly Wiggly, 37
pig pickin', 21
pitmaster, 24, 25, 28, 69
Pitmasters
Anderson, B.R., 133
Cranmore, Teresa, 95
Hughes, Norton, 161
Myers, Adam, 73, 77
Reich, Wade, 37
Robertson, Forrest, 126
Steele, Skip, 63
Turner, Helen, 107
"plate lunch," 50
a meat and three, 50, 84

"Poppos," Gadsden, Alabama, 37
pork rinds, 96, 97
Printup Hotel, Gadsden, Alabama, 37
"Poppos," 37

R

Repast restaurant, 84
"reverse volcano," 23, 24
rotisserie-style smoker, 128

S

San Antonio, 133, 135
San Antonio Spurs, 135
sauces, 27, 28, 29, 30–32
Scorpions minor league soccer team, 135
Seoul, South Korea, 84
Shuler's Bar-B-Que, Latta, South Carolina, 160–169
focus on friends and family, 163
Hamilton, Lorraine (Grin-grin), 162
watermelon cupcake, 162
Hughes, Lynn, 161–163, 166
Hughes, Norton, 161–163, 165
Hughes, Shuler, 161
low and slow, 162, 165
130 foot tall, 40 foot x 80 foot American flag, 161
25-plus-item buffet, 162
Smokehouses
B-Daddy's BBQ, Helotes, Texas, 133
Big Butts BBQ, Leachville, Arkansas, 125
Bogart's Smokehouse, St. Louis, Missouri, 63
Burn Co. BBQ, Tulsa, Oklahoma, 73
Butts To Go, Pell City, Alabama, 37
Heirloom Market BBQ, Atlanta, Georgia, 83
Helen's BBQ, Brownsville, Tennessee, 107
Johnson's Boucanière, Lafayette, Louisiana, 49
Peak Brothers Bar-B-Que, Waverly, Kentucky, 117
Shuler's Bar-B-Que, Latta, South Carolina, 161
Squealer's Hickory Smoked Bar-B-Que, Meridian, Mississippi, 95
Wilber's Barbecue, Goldsboro, North Carolina, 147
smokers 23–24, 25
South Carolina, 29, 33
Southern California, 64
Spain, 95
Squealer's Hickory Smoked Bar-B-Que, Meridian, Mississippi, 94–105
Cranmore, Teresa, 95–98, 100, 103, 104
"My main ingredient is love," 96, 98
Cranmore, Terry, 95–96
pork rinds, 96, 97
Stillwater, Oklahoma, 75
St. Louis, Missouri, 63, 64
Soulard neighborhood, 63
Strong Smoke: mesquite, hickory, oak, pecan, walnut, 25

T

Taming Temperature, 24
Tampa Bay, Florida, 13
Tar Heel magazine, 14
tasso, 56
Tennessee, 29, 125
Terminus, 85
Texas, 29
Texas BBQ, 133, 135

U

University of Alabama, 37
University of Georgia, 27
University of Texas at San Antonio, 133
USA BMX, 133

W

Waverly, Kentucky, 117, 118
Western Kentucky, 118, 120
When Fuel Is Flavor, 25
array of woods and techniques, 25
whole animal cooking, 13
Wilber's Barbecue, Goldsboro, North Carolina, 146–159
Barnes, Margie, 147
Eastern-Carolina tried-and-true traditions, 147
"family table" of regulars, 147
greatest generation, 149
Hill, Fred, 147
longevity is a common theme, 149
Lyerly, Carl, 147
oak coals, 147
open pit, 147
Parks, Leamon, 149
Price, Garry, 149
Radford, Eddie, the "Master Dipper," 148
Shirley, Wilber, or "Boss Hog," 147–150, 155
barbecue "journey" began in '49, 147
"I have been blessed," 149
"I was always told that you never put ketchup on pork, or vinegar on beef," 147, 150
Kenly, North Carolina, 147
whole-hog style of cooking, 147
wood for heat and smoke, 24, 84
alder, 25
apple, 25
avoid any softwoods such as pine, spruce, or cedar, 25
cherry, 25, 68
fresh-cut (green) wood is not ideal, 25
fruit and nut, 25
hardwoods, 25
hickory, 25, 28, 75, 84, 87, 108, 111, 118
maple, 25
mesquite, 25, 28
never use processed lumber, 25
oak, 25, 28, 50, 84, 87, 108, 111, 147
peach, 25
pecan, 25
plum, 25
soaking the wood in water prior to smoking, 25
textures, from dust to pellets to chips to chunks, 25
walnut, 25

A

Appetizers
Antipasto, Dixie, 178
Dips
Loaded Baked Potato Dip, 174
Spicy Queso Dip, 174
Spicy Ranch Dipping Sauce, 181
Petite Sweet Potato Biscuits with Pulled Pork and Slaw, 186
Pickles, Beer-Batter Fried, 181
Pimiento Cheese-Stuffed Pickled Okra, 178
Pork Belly with Soy-Lime Dipping Sauce, Smoked, 194
Sauces
Alabama White Sauce, 190
Buttermilk-Jalapeño Sauce, 191
Buttery Nashville Hot Sauce, 191
Soy-Lime Dipping Sauce, 195
Vietnamese Peanut Sauce, 191
Wing Rub, 193
Wings, Smoked Chicken, 193
Wings, Wonder, 190
Apple Blondie Pie, Caramel, 258
Apple Cider Caramel Sauce, 258

B

Bacon
Candied Bacon, 78
Collards, Bacon and Bourbon, 211
Fatty, 81
Green Beans with Bacon, Sautéed, 208
Hush Puppies, Bacon + Corn, 203
Pork Belly Tonkatsu Ramen, 226
Bananas
Pudding, Fried Banana, 104
Pudding, PB&B, 265
Splits, Grilled Banana, 265
Banh Mi, Down-South, 241
Beans
Baked Beans, Root Beer, 212
Baked Beans, Wade's, 46
Barbecue Beans, 212
BBQ Beans, 122
Green Beans with Bacon, Sautéed, 208
Nachos, Cowboy, 182
Red Beans and Rice, 215
Soup, Bean, 122
Tostadas, Easy Barbecue, 233
Beef
Brisket
B-Daddy's Brisket, 143
Smoked Brisket Pho, 227
Tacos, Brisket, 237
Mac 'n' Cheese, Burnt Ends, 250
Nachos, Cowboy, 182
Pot Pie with Cheese Grits Crust, Barbecue, 245
Tortilla Pie, BBQ, 230
Beer-Can Sticky Chicken, 246
Biscuits, Sweet Potato, 186
Black BBQ Sauce, 32
Blackberry Cobbler, 253
Bologna Sandwich, Smoked, 113
Breads
Biscuits, Sweet Potato, 186
Cornbread, Sweet Potato, 208
Hush Puppies, Bacon + Corn, 203
Brunswick Stew, Chicken, 223
Brunswick Stew, Summer, 223

C

Candied Bacon, 78
Candied Jalapeños, 269
Caramel
Pie, Caramel Apple Blondie, 258
Sauce, Apple Cider Caramel, 258
Sauce, Easy Caramel, 261
Casserole, Squash, 220
Caviar Deviled Eggs, Texas, 179
Chantilly Cream, 253
Cheese
Antipasto, Dixie, 178
Dip, Loaded Baked Potato, 174
Dip, Spicy Queso, 174
Grilled Cheese, Stevie's Stuffed, 55
Grits Crust Batter, Cheese, 245
Lasagna, Pulled Pork Mexican, 249
Mac 'n' Cheese, Burnt Ends, 250
Nachos, Cowboy, 182
Nachos, Redneck Pork, 103
Pimiento Cheese-Stuffed Pickled Okra, 178
Chicken
BBQ Chicken, 157
Beer-Can Sticky Chicken, 246
Brunswick Stew, Chicken, 223
Tostadas, Easy Barbecue, 233
Wings
Dry-Rubbed Smoked Chicken Wings, 45
Smoked Chicken Wings, 193
Wonder Wings, 190
Chips, Rosemary Salt and Vinegar, 173
Chocolate
Cookies, Flourless Peanut Butter-Chocolate Chip, 266
Pie, The Ultimate Chocolate, 259
Whipped Cream, Chocolate, 259
Chowchow, 279
Coleslaw, 111
Coleslaw, Wilber's, 155
Collard Greens, Rice Wine Vinegar and Miso Braised, 93
Condiments. *See also* Pickles; Relishes; Salsa; Sauces.
Candied Jalapeños, 269
Chowchow, 279
Giardiniera, Southern, 275
Pickled Okra, 272
Pico de Gallo, 182
Confetti Slaw, 206
Cookies, Flourless Peanut Butter-Chocolate Chip, 266
Corn
Creamed Corn, 219
Creamed Corn, B-Daddy's Jalapeño, 144
Deep-Fried Corn, 169
Hush Puppies, Bacon + Corn, 203
Relish, Sweet Corn, 279
Smoked Corn, 219
Cornbread, Sweet Potato, 208
Cowboy Nachos, 182
Cucumber and Tomato Salad, Herbed, 200

D

Deep-Fried Corn, 169
Desserts. *See also* Pies and Pastries.
Banana Splits, Grilled, 265
Cookies, Flourless Peanut Butter-Chocolate Chip, 266
Ice Cream, Vanilla, 254
Pudding, Fried Banana, 104
Pudding, PB&B, 265
Sauces
Apple Cider Caramel Sauce, 258

Caramel Sauce, Easy, 261
Chantilly Cream, 253
Chocolate Whipped Cream, 259
Whiskey Whipped Cream, 261
Dip, Peak Brothers, 121
Dressing, Herbed Buttermilk Ranch, 271
Dressing, Slaw, 207

E

Eggs, Texas Caviar Deviled, 179
Eggs, "The Pig Skin" Deviled, 179

G

Giardiniera, Southern, 275
Gingersnap Crust, 263
Greens
Collard Greens, Rice Wine Vinegar and Miso Braised, 93
Collards, Bacon and Bourbon, 211
Grits Crust Batter, Cheese, 245

H

Honey-Soy BBQ Sauce, 246
Hush Puppies, Bacon + Corn, 203

J

Jicama Slaw, 207

K

KB Sauce, 88
Kimchi Base Sauce, 90
Kimchi Pickles, 88
Kimchi Slaw, 90
Korean Pork, Spicy, 87

L

Lasagna, Pulled Pork Mexican, 249
Lemon-Buttermilk Icebox Pie with Gingersnap Crust, Strawberry-, 263
Lime Dipping Sauce, Soy-, 195
Lowcountry Slaw, 206

M

Mac 'n' Cheese, Burnt Ends, 250
Mad Maddie, 70
Mole Barbecue Sauce, 233
Mustard BBQ Sauce, 33
Mustard Vinaigrette, Whole-Grain, 216
Mutton, Peak Brothers Chipped, 120

N

Nachos, Cowboy, 182
Nachos, Redneck Pork, 103

O

Okra
Fries, Spicy Okra, 199
Pickled Okra, 272
Pickled Okra, Pimiento Cheese-Stuffed, 178
Pickled Okra Salsa, 272
Onion Rings, Crispy Fried Sweet, 185
Onions, Pickled Peppers and, 241

P

Peach Cobbler, Easy, 254
Peanut Sauce, Vietnamese, 191
Peanut Butter
Cookies, Flourless Peanut Butter-Chocolate Chip, 266
Pudding, PB&B, 265
Peas
Texas Caviar Deviled Eggs, 179
Peppers
Chipotle Rémoulade, 242
Chipotle Slaw, B-Daddy's, 141
Chipotle Sour Cream, 233
Jalapeño Creamed Corn, B-Daddy's, 144
Jalapeño Sauce, Buttermilk-, 191
Jalapeños, Candied, 269
Pickled Peppers and Onions, 241
Sauce, Chunky Hot, 269
Pickled
Okra, Pickled, 272
Okra, Pimiento Cheese-Stuffed Pickled, 178
Okra Salsa, Pickled, 272
Shallots, Pickled, 217
Pickles
Beer-Batter Fried Pickles, 181
Fire and Ice Pickles, 69
Kimchi Pickles, 88
Pico de Gallo, 182
Pies and Pastries
Blackberry Cobbler, 253
Caramel Apple Blondie Pie, 258
Chocolate Pie, The Ultimate, 259
Crust Batter, Cheese Grits, 245
Crust, Gingersnap, 263
Main Dish
Barbecue Pot Pie with Cheese Grits Crust, 245
BBQ Tortilla Pie, 230
Peach Cobbler, Easy, 254
Strawberry-Lemon-Buttermilk Icebox Pie with Gingersnap Crust, 263
Tennessee Whiskey Pie, 260
Pizza with Pulled Pork, Smoked, 229
Polish Sausage, Smoked, 115
Popcorn, Smoky Barbecue, 173
Pork. *See also* Bacon; Sausage.
Banh Mi, Down-South, 241
Butts
B-Daddy's Pork Butt, 138
Big Butts Pork Butt, 128
Bogart's Pork Butt, 68
Butts To Go Pork Butt, 42
Helen's Pork Butt, 111
Johnson's Boucanière Pork Butt, 55
Pork Butt, 77
Sandwich, Wilber's Pork Butt, 153
Shuler's Pork Butt, 165
Squealer's Pork Butt, 100
Belly Tonkatsu Ramen, Pork, 226
Belly with Soy-Lime Dipping Sauce, Smoked Pork, 194
Deviled Eggs, "The Pig Skin," 179
Korean Pork, Spicy, 87
Nachos, Redneck Pork, 103
Pie, BBQ Tortilla, 230
Pot Pie with Cheese Grits Crust, Barbecue, 245
Pulled Pork and Slaw, Petite Sweet Potato Biscuits with, 186
Pulled Pork Mexican Lasagna, 249
Pulled Pork, Smoked Pizza with, 229
Pulled Pork Tacos, B-Daddy's, 141
Quesadillas, BBQ Pork, 230
Rinds, Deep-Fried Pork, 103
Sandwiches, Southern-Style Cuban, 242
Spaghetti, BBQ, 238
Steak, Big Butts Pork, 131
Tacos, Redneck, 236
Tamales, BBQ Pork, 196
Tostadas, Easy Barbecue, 233
Potatoes. *See also* Sweet Potatoes.
Dip, Loaded Baked Potato, 174
Salad, Grilled Fingerling Potato, 216
Salad, Grilled Potato, 78
Salad, Wilber's Potato, 155
Tots, BBQ, 61
Pudding, Fried Banana, 104
Pudding, PB&B, 265

Q

Quesadillas, BBQ Pork, 230

R

Ramen, Pork Belly Tonkatsu, 226
Redneck Pork Nachos, 103
Redneck Tacos, 236
Relishes
Chowchow, 279

Corn Relish, Sweet, 279
Green Tomato Relish, 278
Pico de Gallo, 182
Rice, Red Beans and, 215
Rinds, Deep-Fried Pork, 103
Rubs
B-Daddy's Butt Rub, 138
Butts To Go Butt Rub, 42
Butts To Go Wing Rub, 45
Greg's Dry Rub, 61
Old-School Butt Rub, 68
Shuler's Butt Rub, 165
Wing Rub, 193

S

Salad Dressings
Herbed Buttermilk Ranch Dressing, 271
Slaw Dressing, 207
Whole-Grain Mustard Vinaigrette, 216
Salads
Herbed Cucumber and Tomato Salad, 200
Potato
Grilled Fingerling Potato Salad, 216
Grilled Potato Salad, 78
Wilber's Potato Salad, 155
Slaws
Chipotle Slaw, B-Daddy's, 141
Coleslaw, 111
Confetti Slaw, 206
Creamy Dill Slaw, 207
Dressing, Slaw, 207
Jicama Slaw, 207
Kimchi Slaw, 90
Lowcountry Slaw, 206
Wilber's Coleslaw, 155
Salsa, Crunchy Summer, 278
Salsa, Pickled Okra, 272
Sandwiches
Banh Mi, Down-South, 241
Chipped Mutton, Peak Brothers, 120
Cuban Sandwiches, Southern-Style, 242
Grilled Cheese, Stevie's Stuffed, 55
Petite Sweet Potato Biscuits with Pulled Pork and Slaw, 186
Polish Sausage, Smoked, 115
Pork Butt, Helen's, 111
Pork Butt Sandwich, Wilber's, 153
Smoked Bologna Sandwich, 113
Smoked Turkey Sandwich, 46
Sauces. *See also* Condiments; Relishes; Salsa.
Alabama White Sauce, 190
Big Butts BBQ Sauce, 128
Black BBQ Sauce, 32
Brown Sugar and Balsamic, 69
Buttermilk-Jalapeño Sauce, 191
Buttery Nashville Hot Sauce, 191
Chipotle Rémoulade, 242
Chipotle Sour Cream, 233
Chunky Hot Sauce, 269
Honey-Soy BBQ Sauce, 246
KB Sauce, 88
Kimchi Base Sauce, 90
Mad Maddie, 70
Mole Barbecue Sauce, 233
Mustard BBQ Sauce, 33
Peak Brothers Dip, 121
Sausage and Tasso Sauce Piquant, 56
Shuler's BBQ Sauce, 165
Sort-of Helen's Sauce, 112
Soy-Lime Dipping Sauce, 195
Spicy Ranch Dipping Sauce, 181
Squealer's Original BBQ Sauce, 100
Sweet BBQ Sauce, 30
Tartar Sauce, 203
Vietnamese Peanut Sauce, 191
Vinegar BBQ Sauce, 30
White BBQ Sauce, 32
Wilber's Vinegar Sauce, 153
Yogurt Sauce, 199
Sausage
Antipasto, Dixie, 178
Fatty, 81
Sauce Piquant, Sausage and Tasso, 56
Smoked Polish Sausage, 115
Shallots, Pickled, 217
Sides. *See also* Salads.
Barbecue Beans, 212
BBQ Beans, 122
Collard Greens, Rice Wine Vinegar and Miso Braised, 93
Collards, Bacon and Bourbon, 211
Creamed Corn, 219
Deep-Fried Corn, 169
Fried Green Tomatoes, 200
Fried Sweet Onion Rings, Crispy, 185
Green Beans with Bacon, Sautéed, 208
Hush Puppies, Bacon + Corn, 203
Pickles, Fire and Ice, 69
Pickles, Kimchi, 88
Red Beans and Rice, 215
Root Beer Baked Beans, 212
Smoked Corn, 219
Spicy Okra Fries, 199
Squash Casserole, 220
Sweet Potato Soufflé, 166
Tots, BBQ, 61
Slow Cooker
B-Daddy's Jalapeño Creamed Corn, 144
Brisket Tacos, 237
Snacks
Chips, Rosemary Salt and Vinegar, 173
Popcorn, Smoky Barbecue, 173
Soups
Bean Soup, 122
Smoked Brisket Pho, 227
Soy-Lime Dipping Sauce, 195
Spaghetti, BBQ, 238
Squash Casserole, 220
Strawberry-Lemon-Buttermilk Icebox Pie with Gingersnap Crust, 263
Sweet Potatoes
Biscuits, Sweet Potato, 186
Cornbread, Sweet Potato, 208
Soufflé, Sweet Potato, 166

T

Tacos
Brisket Tacos, 237
Pulled Pork Tacos, B-Daddy's, 141
Redneck Tacos, 236
Tamales, BBQ Pork, 196
Tartar Sauce, 203
Tasso Sauce Piquant, Sausage and, 56
Tomatoes
Fried Green Tomatoes, 200
Green Tomato Relish, 278
Pico de Gallo, 182
Salad, Herbed Cucumber and Tomato, 200
Tonkatsu Ramen, Pork Belly, 226
Tortilla Pie, BBQ, 230
Tostadas, Easy Barbecue, 233
Turkey Sandwich, Smoked, 46

V

Vanilla Ice Cream, 254
Vegetables. *See also* specific types.
Brunswick Stew, Summer, 223
Chowchow, 279
Giardiniera, Southern, 275
Slaw, Confetti, 206

W

Whiskey Whipped Cream, 261
White BBQ Sauce, 32
Wings
Chicken Wings, Dry-Rubbed Smoked, 45
Rub, Wing, 193
Smoked Chicken Wings, 193
Wonder Wings, 190